Creative Optimum Self

Transform Your Life and Your World

Costantino Delli

Dedication

I dedicate this book to the silent and powerful voice that lives inside us all. I know who you are. My wish is that each of you connects to that same inner voice—it is your Creative Optimum Self (COS).

When you are connected and live from your COS, you experience an infinite abundance of love, compassion, and gratitude for a more Loving, Inspiring, Fulfilling Existence (LIFE).

In that state, you discover not only your potential, but also your responsibility to shape a better world for everyone.

Gratitude

My warmest gratitude goes out to all my family, friends, clients, authors, poets, actors, filmmakers, and to people I have met whose names I never knew.

Thank you for your inspiration. It is through these experiences that this book emerged.

To all of you who have found The Way and are living from your Creative Optimum Self, thank you for your continued inspiration.

To my "home," New York City—for all the experiences and lessons over the years—and to sunny Southern California, for reminding me of my birthplace and inspiring me to complete this book.

Special thanks to Leonard Riggio, Edward Ash-Milby, and everyone at Barnes & Noble for your dedication and support.

Mom, thank you for the guidance and unconditional love over the years. Your strength and courage are an inspiration to all.

Tanya, thank you for always challenging and supporting me to complete this book.

And special gratitude to Bianco, the wise Pekingese, who taught me how to live in the moment, and to Merlin, the adopted Russian Blue—a teacher of life and a great typist.

TABLE OF CONTENTS

A Word Before You Begin (2026)

It seems like yesterday that I sat down to write this book. Nineteen years have passed since I wrote the words you're holding now, and time has a way of moving faster than we realize.

This book is for those who sense—quietly or urgently—that there is more to life than productivity, roles, or survival. It is for individuals who want to live with clarity and integrity, not by adopting another belief system, but by reconnecting with their own inner intelligence. It is for leaders, parents, creators, professionals, and thoughtful seekers who feel called to integrate who they are with how they live, work, and relate. If you are drawn to a way of being that is grounded, humane, and deeply practical—and if you are willing to look inward with honesty—this book is written for you.

When I began writing what is now titled *Creative Optimum Self: Transform Your Life and Your World*—originally published as *The Way: Live Your Dream, It's Not a Secret!*—I was driven by a simple but urgent desire: to share a practice that had already changed my life. The original title was intentional. At the time, *The Secret* had just captured public attention, and a buyer at Barnes & Noble encouraged me to position my book alongside that conversation. My message moved in a different direction. I wasn't offering a mystery or a hidden formula. I believed—and still do—that living your dream is not a secret at all. It is practical, grounded, and accessible when you commit to the Inner and Outer Steps described in these pages. That belief shaped both the title and the tone of the book.

The book was born from experience, not theory. For years before I wrote it, I had been living these practices quietly and consistently. At a certain point, I felt compelled to put them into words. I wrote as if I were sitting across from you, having a conversation. The language is simple, organic, and direct because I wanted it to feel personal—almost as if you were reading my private journal. This was never meant to be a manual. It is a practice shared in trust.

Everything about its creation was accelerated. I wrote the first draft in three weeks. Within a few months, the book was available through Barnes & Noble and Amazon. I published it through my own company, printing 2,500 hardcover copies. I didn't pursue traditional marketing or promotion. Life was full, work was demanding, and I allowed the book to simply exist on its own, without pushing it into the world.

The response was immediate and overwhelmingly positive. I shared copies freely, donated many, and today only a handful of those original hardcovers remain. What stayed with me most was a particular review that dismissed the book as unrealistic, even nonsensical. An Amazon reviewer took issue with the ideas that we are deeply connected, that we move together through space, and that we are part of a larger whole—what I referred to then as "the Universe."

I remember that review clearly because of what happened afterward. In the years that followed, I began to hear the same language everywhere. In leadership conversations. In neuroscience. In wellness, philosophy, and culture at large. Ideas that once sounded fringe had entered the mainstream. Concepts that were questioned in 2007 were now widely accepted and discussed. Even though only 2,500 physical copies of this book existed, its message seemed to return to me through countless voices and mediums—reflecting back in ways I could never have planned. That reflection is one of the reasons this book is being re-released now—as I continue to see these ideas echoed and expanded across the world today.

Another reason arrived more recently, and unexpectedly. A few months ago, I watched a film starring George Clooney, and near the end there is a scene that stopped me completely. The character is in a movie theater, watching scenes from his movies unfold on the screen. He is both the subject and the audience. I recognized the moment immediately. That scene mirrors an exercise I describe in this book—one offered as part of the Outer Steps, particularly in the context of being warm, gracious, and conscious in how we move through the world. I wrote about the idea that we are all the central character in our own lives, and at the same time, the observer. That when we learn to watch our own lives as if they were a film, something shifts. We become more intentional. More kind. More awake. Every interaction begins to matter—not because we are performing, but because we are present. Seeing that idea expressed clearly, years later, through a different medium, felt like another quiet confirmation. Whether or not it was inspired by anything I wrote is beside the point. What mattered was the resonance. The work was still alive.

The third reason for this update is more personal. I wanted to share how this book has shaped my life. When I recently sat down and read it again, I was struck by how genuine the language still feels. The voice hasn't aged, and the message hasn't faded. This practice never left me. It became embedded in how I live.

When I wrote this book, I was already living from the practice I had come to call the Creative Optimum Self. For nearly a decade before writing these pages, I had been applying these principles quietly and consistently in my own life—learning to observe, aligning inner awareness with outer action, and listening more deeply to the intelligence within. Writing the book was simply the moment when that lived experience finally found its way onto the page.

Over time, that practice deepened and matured. What began as a disciplined way of living gradually revealed itself as something more integrated—an awareness that was not only guiding my actions, but shaping how

I experienced life itself. Only later did I recognize that this embodied way of living—rooted in awareness, presence, and alignment—was operating as a form of inner intelligence that I now call **Integrated Being Intelligence**. What I once described as becoming the "eyes and ears of the Universe," a phrase that concludes Chapter Ten, gradually shifted from an aspiration into a lived awareness. What once felt like seeking gently matured into witnessing.

Today, I understand that awareness differently—as awareness of awareness itself. My relationship with what I once called "the Universe" has expanded. I now see it as the seen dimension within a larger field that includes both the visible and the unseen. We exist as part of an infinite intelligence, operating as the Creative Optimum Self in both dimensions, continuously integrating inner and outer worlds. That realization completes the language of this book and deepens its meaning.

The practices described here remain practical and grounded. Journaling, reflection, and intentional action remain powerful tools. What has evolved is how I engage with them. Where I once wrote extensively, I now visualize. Where I once documented experience, I now observe it directly, watching life unfold in scenes from a wider vantage point. That evolution eventually led me to write a second book, *48 Answers for My Son: An Architecture of Integrated Leadership Intelligence*—

a work that also carries a cinematic dimension in how the story of a life unfolds.

This book remains the foundation of that journey. What you are about to read reflects exactly where I was—and it still holds. Creative Optimum Self is the unifying field of awareness. Integrated Being Intelligence describes how that awareness is lived internally through presence and embodiment, and **Integrated Leadership Intelligence** describes how the same intelligence expresses itself outwardly through action, service, and responsibility.

Today, these Inner and Outer Steps matter more than ever. We live in an age of constant notification, acceleration, and distraction—where attention is fragmented and grounding is rare. The Inner Steps described in this book were designed to do exactly that: to bring you back into yourself. Through solitude, reflection, time in nature, care for the body, and exposure to ideas that elevate rather than deplete, you begin to peel away layers that are not essential.

From that grounding, the Outer Steps emerge naturally. Efficiency replaces urgency. Relationships deepen. Gratitude becomes lived rather than performed. You begin to move through the world with warmth, clarity, and responsibility—because presence shapes the quality of every action. Even today's most powerful tools, including artificial intelligence, can serve this evolution when used consciously. When approached with intention, they reflect wisdom and mirror the quality of our awareness as it matures. In that sense, the practice you are about to read is timeless—and uniquely suited for the world we are now navigating.

At a time when everything appears more connected on the surface, this work invites a deeper understanding of what that connection truly means. Beneath the visible networks and shared systems is a more fundamental integration—one that begins within. When that inner coherence is recognized and lived, clarity replaces fragmentation, and the way we think, act, and relate begins to align naturally.

That is why this work returns now—with greater relevance, greater urgency, and a renewed invitation to live from your Creative Optimum Self.

Foreword

Every so often there comes along a person, event, or book that changes people's lives. One of those people was born in Taranto, Italy, and moved with his family to the United States eight years later.

Costantino was always a "unique" child—never afraid to stand for what is right and always the performer. Both his parents were very hard workers, which often left Cos—a nickname he adopted later in life—to entertain himself through his imagination. He could create an entire game of soccer with nothing more than a brick wall and a ball. In his imagination, it became a field with twenty-two players and stands full of screaming fans.

He always found a solution, a way to make things better. A perfect example of this is Cos's first "job"—delivering espresso in his native Italy. He was only five years old. He noticed that when the customer received it, the espresso was not creamy or as hot as it should be. Not one of the clients complained; however, just in their reaction and through his own observations, Cos knew this was not perfect or optimal. What did he do? On the next delivery he covered the espresso with a saucer and presto. A very satisfied customer.

Why did I share such a simple story with you?

This is a perfect example of how he sees the world—he only wants the best from himself and all of us and he recognizes an opportunity or potential for greatness in even the smallest of circumstances. Whether as simple as espresso or as complex as a multi-billion-dollar initiative, he approaches every situation the same way—through clarity, efficiency, and quality execution. Without efficiency and quality action in our lives, the world becomes cluttered with unfinished details and "loose ends," making everyday living feel unnecessarily heavy.

Costantino offers a way to eliminate the clutter and live from your Creative Optimum Self. Through a simple, ten step process you can also live from your greatest self. I know this because I am living proof. I was at a point in my life where I felt happy, successful, and fulfilled. At this time, I began to share with a unique and selfless individual who made me realize that I did not know myself as well as I thought. He saw a light in me—a potential that I never knew existed.

Costantino is passionate in spreading this wisdom enabling organizations, businesses, and individuals to tap into their own potential. His energy and enthusiasm are genuine and contagious. I have seen him create "magic" through truth and wisdom, something we all have the ability to do. He is tenacious in working towards creating a better world for all by sharing his journey, successes, disappointments, and unending curiosity to learn more from everyone he encounters.

Since that time, I have continued connecting with my greatest self. I have tapped into my creativity and can see the dramatic changes in my life, personally and professionally. As I continue to integrate these steps daily and share my own success stories, I know they inspire others to do the same.

The pages before you will transform your life and influence those around you. Embrace them. Live them. Love them.

They have certainly changed mine.

—Tanya Perrin

Introduction

This book is designed to guide you toward living your greatest life.

I was inspired to write it after years of debate with friends and clients about whether people would be interested in reading *The Way*.

I have dedicated my entire life to personal transformation, and through my consulting practice guiding businesses, organizations, and communities to transform or improve. Like many of you, I have lived an exciting, ever-changing life, full of ups and downs and, above all, with passion. What I am most passionate about is transformation in all forms—nature, personal, business, and community. I feel a deep sense of exhilaration when I observe an individual, an environment, or a living being transform into something greater. There is great beauty in this observation and it brings me an abundance of joy. I thought I was satisfied continuing on this path using the steps outlined in this book, but in the last six months, I have been hearing the universe, through all its forms, speak to me, urging me to write and share this book with all of you.

Each day friends, clients, and strangers share with me that we live in a world of injustice, suffering, anger, and disappointment. Through these conversations I have also seen something else emerge: a growing awareness that there is a more grounded and meaningful way to live.

The final push that I needed to complete this book was when I attended an International Forum, chaired by Deepak Chopra. The forum was held to connect leaders from organizations, businesses, and communities and share the contributions they are making to bring unity and transformation in the world. During the session, Deepak asked each of us to complete what he called a "soul profile." This profile consisted of several questions about who we are, our passions and what contributions we wish to make to the world. He suggested that as we share who we are on the inside, we can learn more about each other and see if we can make connections, support one another, and leverage our work. I connected with the questions and realized that I needed to share this with the rest of you. I realized that life would not allow me to move forward until I completed this.

The Way is organized into steps divided into two parts that I call the Inner and Outer Steps. The Outer Steps are based on five principles that I have successfully used in my professional career. These principles are customized as needed, serving the client to execute a strategy to advance and transform their business. For example, building solid relationships across all business units, leveraging what works, and implementing processes that are efficient and encourage creative thinking. These principles, when properly aligned and executed, bring about change, improvement, and transformation. The key to success is always proper execution, not only in business but, as you will see, also in personal transformation.

Every day I am reminded by my personal clients, friends, and everyday people how difficult it is to execute or follow through with something. People know what they need to do: eat less or exercise to lose weight, stop the excessive drinking, get out of a toxic relationship or get a better job. But for various reasons, they are not able to get started or stay on a consistent path. While many books on the market today offer knowledge and experience, few offer a simple, organized guide that inspires and empowers people to execute and remain consistent. By tapping into the business success stories that I and my clients have experienced, I will share with you the five Outer Steps that will bring success to you in all aspects of your life and guide you to your Creative Optimum Self or COS.

The Inner Steps discussed are based on my personal experiences, science and the arts. These steps have always been part of my life, even though at times I may have neglected a few of the steps. For instance, as a child I always enjoyed sharing time with nature and in solitude but never felt lonely. When I began reading and writing poetry in my 20s, I knew that through nature and silence I was tapping into an inner source for inspiration.

When I began studying professional acting in New York City and reading classic books, Constantin Stanislavski's—*An Actor Prepares*, I realized the connection between overall well-being to inspiration. Acting and poetry teach that your body is a vessel or an instrument and if you treat it well, you will tap into an unlimited source of inspiration. For most people, this becomes the most challenging aspect of transformation to connect with this source, but once you have access to it, you can live from this place in each moment, and your life will begin to change in ways you can feel and measure.

I will guide you through the Inner Steps and over time as you practice, you will live from your Creative Optimum Self, and as you incorporate both the Inner and Outer Steps, you will inspire others to tap into their own wisdom and transform as well. By following this path together, we can help make our world a better place.

Guarantee

I am confident that by incorporating the Inner and Outer Steps outlined in this book into your daily life, you will experience meaningful and measurable improvements over time. Many people begin to notice changes within a few months; for others, the process unfolds more gradually.

The Inner Steps can feel more challenging at first, especially if this kind of self-observation and reflection is unfamiliar. Peeling away accumulated layers takes patience, and the steps may need to be adapted to individual circumstances. This is not a sign of failure—it is part of the process.

My commitment to you is simple: read this book with honesty, complete the exercises, and integrate the Inner and Outer Steps into your daily life. When approached with sincerity and consistency, meaningful change begins to take shape. If, after ninety days you are unable to observe measurable improvement, reach out to me with your specific situation. I will offer a complimentary session to explore how you can reconnect with your Creative Optimum Self.

Before we begin this journey, there are two things we need to do. Sign an agreement and complete an assessment. Let's evaluate your body and current emotional state to measure and track your progress at any time during this journey.

Agreement

I know it is easy for all of us to say we will do something and then, for various reasons, fail to follow through on our plan. But I also know that writing is powerful and when we put it in writing, it takes a deeper meaning. It becomes an agreement—it sits in front of you and reminds you of the promises you made to yourself.

Today is _____________ and I,__________________ of my own free will, agree to be open and consider the steps and guidelines set forth in this book.

My intention is to inspire you, in a harmonious way, to execute these steps on your own, not to force you into something you do not want to do. Give it a try, be reasonable and commit to it for a few months. As you follow the steps creatively, you will become more aware of yourself and life around you, and over time, you will notice a meaningful shift in how you relate to yourself and others.

This assessment will help you establish a baseline for your emotional state, physical well-being, and daily habits, allowing you to observe your progress as you move through this practice.

Assessment

Now that you have agreed to consider this path, take a moment to answer the following questions and record the results.

1.   Date and time of this assessment.

2.   Your body measurements: weight, height, waist, hip, chest size, body fat.

3.   Measure or ask your doctor to take your blood pressure.

4.   Determine your cholesterol level through blood work, if available.

Answer yes or no to the following questions:

5.   Do you feel lethargic at times?

6.   Do you get headaches or stomachaches at times?

7. Do you feel foggy at times?

8. Do you find yourself always eating or munching?

9. Do you think you enjoy your food or do you rush through it?

10. Do you feel heavy after eating a meal?

11. Do you feel sad or lonely at times?

12. Do you get angry or get upset easily at times?

13. Do you think you have a temper or are quick to judge things at times?

14. Do you worry, have fears or anxiety, or experience stress at times?

15. Do you feel an emptiness inside of you?

.

16. What is your definition of a spirit?

17. Do you think that

(1) You are a human being who sometimes has spiritual experiences

or

(2) You are a spiritual being living a human life at this moment?

18. What is your passion?

And lastly, write down how you feel before you begin, and again after reading the book in one sitting?

Once you have recorded this initial assessment, use it as a baseline as you progress on this journey and compare it each time you complete the assessment.

Okay, you are now ready to begin this journey of transformation.

This is my life practice.

Transformation
begins each new day.

PART I

Transformation

Transformation is taking place all around us. I define transformation as bringing "light" into a person, living being, event, situation, environment, organization, and ultimately the world. This light can be manifested through efficiency, order, joy, peace, harmony, or love, just to name a few. Many people are doing great work in various ways around the world to make this world a more loving and peaceful place for everyone. But some are not aware how their work is having a positive impact and others do not think that their help is needed. A great many people have simply given up on this world; they believe decline is inevitable—there is violence, war, terror, poverty, and disease everywhere. We are reminded of this each day.

It is true that there exists much suffering in this world, but because suffering exists today, it is not a given that it will exist tomorrow. Society has a tendency to accept limitation as reality—embracing the belief that 'this is just the way it is,' and that it cannot be changed. Society tells us that we are different from one another—we have different religions, political beliefs, cultures; we look different, we carry different labels and needs— and from this perspective, even conflict and violence are often accepted as inevitable. We disagree, we argue, and someone always wins; "that's just the way it is."

My experiences in life have taught me otherwise. We can live a life where we celebrate our differences with compassion, learn from our mistakes through our experience, and gain wisdom by taking responsibility for our actions. I have learned that beyond our differences, there is a common ground that we all walk on. Some people understand this but are hesitant to practice it in their lives because they are afraid to be judged by society while a few understand this, live by it, and make their contribution in transforming the world. Many people are not aware of this, or are not conscious of it at this time.

By becoming aware of these steps and incorporating them into your life, you will experience a shift in awareness. You will become more curious about life and it will push you to grow, evolve, and reconnect with your Creative Optimum Self.

You are now ready to begin the work of transformation—starting from within.

Chapter One

Transformation Is Everywhere

Transformation is all around us—in business, in nature, from a sunrise to a sunset, from rain turning into the water we drink, flowers blooming, the birth of life—and in personal transformation: anger turning to joy, the realization of a dream, reaching a goal, finding a solution, evolving into a wiser person. Over time, I have realized that I am most passionate about personal transformation because of the knowledge and wisdom that can be gained through experience.

I was born in Taranto, Italy, a beautiful, ancient, southern city in the Apulia region. My parents operated a neighborhood café that served coffee, pastries, and pizza in the newer part of town. I loved my childhood—it was spent between playing soccer in the parking lots and on the beach, spending time in the café helping out my dad at the cash register, and going to school. At age five, I had the first big change in my life. I almost died from a simple appendix operation. Imagine this: the top doctor in the city operated on me while intoxicated and forgot to untie my intestine after removing my appendix. For three days, I was not well—white as a ghost in the hospital and could not eat, drink or move. According to the experts, it was all considered normal after such an operation. If it weren't for my mom's tenacity, I would not be writing to you today. She persisted until she got the eyes and ears of a true expert, visiting from Switzerland, to have a look at me. He said he would do what he can and asked my mom if she was a woman of great faith, which she was. I was then back on the operating table and I remember lying underneath these huge lamps and thinking to myself, is this the end? Where will I go? But, somehow I knew that I would be OK, I was not afraid. The surgery was a success and after a long recovery I was happy to be home.

A few years later, my parents decided to visit family we had in America, in Trenton, NJ. My mom and I visited the great land of "opportunity." I was not happy to leave home but my mom convinced me that it would be an adventure to visit a new place. But my first experience on a plane made me very nervous—it was huge, and I wondered what language these people were speaking.

When we finally landed at Kennedy Airport, there was a snow blizzard, first time I experienced snow in my life. It was beautiful to look at, but the cold was too much for a Southern beach boy. It was not easy to adjust and after a few trips back and forth, my mom and dad decided to leave the beautiful and warm Taranto for the industrial capital city, Trenton. Talk about contrasts.

The personal transformation stories keep coming as I will share with you. Transformation is all around us—

it is part of life, and if there are parts of life that are not in harmony, we can change them by becoming more aware of ourselves and those around us. If you pause and look closely at your own life, you will begin to see that transformation is already taking place. Not only within your body and mind, but through your experiences, your relationships, and what you are creating each day. Much of it happens quietly—often without recognition—but it is there.

By becoming aware of it, you begin to participate in it more consciously. And that is where true transformation begins.

peel away layers, and you will see
beauty in all things

Chapter Two

Peel Away Layers

Society has a practice of teaching us that if we follow religious or political rules and laws, we will be good citizens—and if we are really good, we can go to some form of heaven. In a way, society has taken on this responsibility to take care of or control us by informing us of what we need to do to live a happy life. But our soul already knows how to live a joyous life; many people, however, are not connected to it anymore.

This book guides you toward discovering your inner truth, your Creative Optimum Self. We need to remove some of what our ancestors have taught us from religions, cultures, and traditions, and replace them with the wisdom and knowledge already contained within each of us. This wisdom has always existed. Indeed, if you read ancient documents, poetry, essays across many philosophies and religions, you will notice a common theme. They all share experiences that are divine, miraculous, and discuss the light, harmony, peace, and love. They existed then, and they exist today. Like the Bible written centuries ago, one can be written today, filled with parables and passages from our modern experiences.

At a deeper level, the essential truths of life have always existed—and remain unchanged. But it is easy to forget this, given the leaps and bounds we have made in technology, which can become a distraction from the true nature of reality. We should use technology to enrich our lives and make things easier, while remaining grounded in the deeper reality of our lives. Society has taught us that we, human beings, are not perfect. We are only human—this reflects a limited way of seeing ourselves, where we begin to justify our constraints rather than recognize our potential. The human body is inherently intelligent and responsive; it is our conditioned thinking that often introduces limitation. When we live in alignment with our deeper awareness, the body naturally supports balance, vitality, and the expression of life. And if you live from the soul today, you can create the life you wish to live.

How can you begin to live from your soul? You begin by removing the "layers," past beliefs and false notions that have become part of everyday life. As you remove the layers and peel away years of disappointments, angers, fears, and anxieties, you will find your soul inside. This soul is beautiful, safe, and a guide that will enrich your life. The soul speaks through your inner awareness and through others—friends and strangers. This same intelligence lives everywhere, and it is only natural to hear the universe speak to you. You need to be present, alert, and listen from the soul to hear it. You need to be "clean" from past false beliefs. This is difficult for many because we pile up stuff in our heads and stay attached to them.

But there is a way. When you execute the Inner Steps—beginning with journaling, as discussed later—you will experience greater clarity in your mind and live more fully in the present. From this place of awareness, you will gain greater authorship of your life and begin shaping the kind of life you truly wish to live. This shift begins when we move beyond limiting ways of seeing ourselves and recognize our capacity to choose and take responsibility for our path.

We have been raised in a world that often reinforces patterns of limitation in how people see themselves. And as a result, this creates layers, inefficiencies, and blocks us from living the life we were born to live. A limited mindset is not always obvious. There is a quieter, more subtle pattern that can create just as much strain in life. It appears when people accept limitation as fate—believing they are not passionate, not gifted, or not capable of excellence simply because they were "not born that way." They may begin to feel unworthy, even though that perception does not reflect their true nature.

Over time, some people begin to accept this way of living—they tell themselves that they are not capable of being happy, optimal, or a light. They may begin to act in ways that reinforce these beliefs, and society sometimes nourishes this by unintentionally supporting the behavior. Hence, you have those who have addictions like alcohol and drugs and these actions are supported—"he is this way because of his addiction." Instead, they should be guided to recognize that their actions may be causing pain and suffering to themselves and to those around them. They can be guided toward meaningful action—seeking support, having honest conversations with trusted people, learning through books and reflection, and following a structured path such as the one outlined here.

We are citizens of the world, and as citizens, we have a responsibility to be the "eyes and ears of the universe." That is, we are called to be protectors of the whole. We do this by living in a way that creates harmony and love in the world, while gently guiding others beyond patterns that keep them disconnected from their potential.

At the same time, this path is rooted in compassion. Supporting and uplifting those who seek help remains essential—especially those who have momentarily lost their way. We are here to offer empathy, understanding, and encouragement, helping others reconnect with their inner wisdom. They carry within them the capacity for happiness and transformation, and with the right support, that potential can be realized. When we live and support others in this way, we create an environment where people feel empowered to take ownership of their lives and evolve.

Transformation can take place when we are aware—at times this is not easy. I have had many struggles in my life, and I observe that many others experience the same. The key is to recognize this and become aware, allowing change to begin. This awareness can guide you to take steps that will bring positive changes to your life over time. Living with wisdom and knowledge is the only true way to exist—and it begins with understanding how you relate to yourself.

Most people look outward when seeking change, trying to adjust circumstances, environments, or others around them. Yet lasting transformation begins within. It requires the willingness to turn inward with honesty, courage, and compassion. At times, this inner work may feel uncomfortable. There may be memories, emotions, or patterns that surface. This is part of the process. When approached with patience and awareness, what once felt heavy begins to loosen, and clarity begins to emerge.

As your relationship with yourself deepens, your outer world begins to reflect that change. Your actions become more intentional, your responses more grounded, and your presence more aligned. From this place, transformation is no longer something you chase—it becomes something you live.

The Way to your COS is like scuba diving—
the deeper you go,
the more beautiful the pearl you discover

Chapter Three

The Way with Your COS

What is The Way?

Throughout ancient traditions, The Way, or Tao, is described as a way of living aligned with the universe. The Way is how to live a life of peace, love, and pure bliss. Your COS is The Way.

It is The Way that provides what you need to live an optimum, creative life. It is easy to be happy when everything goes well—but how can you remain happy at all times, especially during disappointments, failures, and losses in life? How can this be possible? Many people think that it is not realistic that this world can adopt a utopia even after many wonderful leaders, poets and religious figures have tried the same before. The fact that these inspirational people have lived in the past is proof that this is possible. They have advanced our civilization through their books, teachings and actions. Books can be inspirational, but transformation happens through execution.

In my business and personal experiences, this is the biggest challenge for individuals to follow through on great ideas. I have dedicated my entire life to guiding others to learn the art of execution. My intention for this book is to inspire and empower you to execute the

COS Inner and Outer Steps and observe how you can transform into your greatest self—and how you engage with the world.

The COS steps are based on the knowledge that we are spiritual beings who live in physical bodies for this moment. This spiritual being—the soul within you—naturally seeks expression, but if your physical body, or ego, becomes absorbed by societal layers, it can get in the way and the soul cannot fully express itself. If it does not live, then you lose your true self. Thus, it becomes very important to keep the layers away by removing sources of negativity from your life—toxic people, situations, and environments. When we do this, we achieve peace and tranquility and can hear the soul again. Once we hear the soul, we begin to recognize our connection to the universal flow—the source of all good things. This voice is who we are. We are all one and belong to the same source. We have different physical identities, yet each soul rises from the same source. If we can all live from the soul, then we will achieve harmony and unity. This is the direct path to your Creative Optimum Self.

Once the basic principles of these COS steps are embraced and practiced daily, you will transform your life and inspire others to do the same. Upon executing the steps, you will enjoy greater health in all areas of your life—body, mind, spirit, careers, relationships, and finances. Are you ready to transform your life?

These steps are simple and practical. They are not based on any religion or political beliefs. You do not need any special skills or education to practice them. As you incorporate them into your daily life, as naturally as you breathe, you will connect with the inner guide and over time you will be more aware of yourself and those around you. We all have choices and the choice we make today determines the life we will have tomorrow. And if we want to have a better world tomorrow, we need to start today, wherever we are and whatever we are doing.

The first five steps focus on you. Some people may find this challenging as they are not accustomed to placing attention on themselves—they were not raised this way, or they are afraid to address their fears, or think that it is a selfish act to think of oneself. But only when you truly know yourself, and you live from your soul, can you help others. Incorporate these simple, practical steps into your daily life and you will see yourself in a new wonderful way.

The last five steps focus on how you interact with the rest of the world. If you practice the Inner Steps daily, you will naturally evolve into the Outer Steps and inspire others to do the same. You will be living proof that the world can indeed be governed by peace, love, and harmony. Be open, complete the exercises that follow each step, and allow your imagination to guide you through this journey.

Transforming your life
is a journey worth taking.

PART II

Transform Your Life

Before continuing, it may help to orient yourself to the journey you are about to take.

Creative Optimum Self is the unifying field of this work—the state of being that emerges when inner awareness and outer life become aligned. The first five steps cultivate Integrated Being Intelligence: the lived intelligence of the body, emotions, mind, relationships, and connection to Source. The last five steps express that same intelligence outwardly in the world—through responsibility, service, and how you relate, decide, and lead—Integrated Leadership Intelligence.

These are not separate paths, but two expressions of one consciously lived life. Now that you have explored what transformation truly means, we can begin the work of transforming your life through five Inner Steps that guide you to connect with your Creative Optimum Self: journaling, meditation, inspirational reading, nature and solitude, and well-being. I recommend going through the steps in order the first time, then revisiting specific ones in more detail. Please pace yourself and don't rush through it. Be patient and kind to yourself.

Inner Steps reflect ancient wisdom
for the personal and universal soul

Chapter Four

Inspiration for Inner Steps

The Inner Steps are based on my personal life experiences, the arts, and sciences.

Journaling is the first step. I began keeping a journal at a very young age in my life. I was six years old in Italy and in first grade. Our teacher introduced us to recording a daily chronicle in our notebooks—the homework each night was to write about our day. I was very consistent in writing in my notebook and kept it when my family moved from Italy to the United States. For the next four years, we resided in several different residences until we finally purchased a home. During the move, I lost my notebooks, which made me very sad because they meant a great deal to me. I stopped writing on a regular basis and would only write when I experienced a crisis in my life, like my father's passing or when I reached a low point in my life years later. Then I decided to start a new journal and record the major events of my life from my first early memories.

The primary reason that I write into my journal daily is that it keeps me grounded. I learn a great deal about myself by writing how I feel on a particular day or the impact experiences are having in my life. As I write in my journal, I find solutions to problems. It guides me on how to interact with other people and deal with situations and provides me with insight and wisdom about life in general. It also allows my creative side to awaken, thus the emergence of the following poem—

Live in the Moment

In the moment, a circle of light will shine from above.

This light will keep you focused and light up your surroundings, so that you can see.

When you can see, you are in the moment. The present.

When you are in the present, you are the light.

The light is within you.

The beauty of nature that I see with my eyes is still present within when my eyes are shut.

I know where I am but I could be anywhere, I see the images of life before me and I know my eyes are closed.

I feel the breeze of spring days sweep by me and I know that today is fall.

I touch the thin air that fills the sky, still I can see nature from up above.

I know why I come here even when I do not recognize this place.

I sit by the waters and wait for life to come to me.

I hear the wind passing through me leaving me with the seeds of life's secrets.

I taste the sweet juices of the seeds as they travel deep in my soul.

I feel the unfertilized beings from the womb of creation and cradle them in my lips.

I plant the seeds of my future, in the eternal place of timeless awareness.

I see the beautiful seeds resting in silence close to me.

I see my unbound destiny unravel from the resting seed.

As the light turns to darkness, I awaken and find myself resting above.

I know I have been here before but I don't know when.

As I sit under an oak tree by the lake, I observe nature expressing its beauty.

I see the sun warming the still water. I feel the breeze sweeping the flowers with ecstasy.

I hear the birds singing and dancing freely, I touch the source of all creation, love.

I know now that I come here often.

It is silent, it is peaceful, it is still.

It is a place of haven; it is my place, and I can always find it in my heart.

Writing is also part of the life of a professional actor. Like many actors, I began performing at the young age of five for my family and friends. Then as an adult, I studied professionally and learned a great deal about the link between the acting process and life. What I love and appreciate about acting is the overall process of bringing a character to life. And part of the process is to do research, study and write about the character. You learn a great deal about the character by writing out the likes and dislikes—what he likes to wear, what his fears are and his dreams. Over time an actor will create the psyche of the character and will use this outline to shape his performance. And this is the connection to journaling—writing becomes a useful tool for an actor to prepare for a performance. Journaling is the first inner step—it is the starting point for change.

Meditation is the second inner step. I was raised Roman Catholic and prayer was part of my daily routine. I prayed like the church taught us and what I remember most about praying as a child was that it always brought me peace afterwards. Over the years, prayer has evolved into a form of meditation that I practice now which is very different from the early days. Still, the outcome of my meditation is peace. I use meditation to tap into my silence and source of inspiration and what emerges is a beautiful piece of life that fuels my day.

The third inner step is inspirational reading. My soul is awakened and inspired by reading material that stirs emotion, stimulate my inner senses and intellect. It takes me away from my daily routine and brings me back refreshed and ready to deal with life. This third inner step will bring you closer to reach your inner wisdom.

Nature and solitude is the fourth inner step. Ever since I was a child, I always enjoyed spending time with nature. I grew up very close to the beach and it became my favorite past time, to swim, play, and build sand castles. I always felt safe and protected, not only during the day, also at night walking under the stars. My parents would take us every night for a walk along the beautiful beachfront promenade in Taranto. I remember walking and holding my father's hand and looking up to the stars and counting them in an imaginary square I created in the sky. I would usually fall asleep and my father had to carry me home and I always felt refreshed. Today, spending time with nature remains a big part of my life. Even a short walk through the park or by a lake can be a welcomed time out during a busy day.

The same is true for spending time alone, whether or not it takes place with nature. I love sharing time with all kinds of people but at times I do enjoy spending time with my own thoughts. As a poet or actor, this is also the case. I write my best work if I am alone watching a sunset or looking at a river, the sea, or the mountains. Even in solitude you can still feel a connection with friends, family and everyone.

Well-being is the fifth and final inner step. When I was a child, my eating habits were determined more by my parents, the Italian culture and their traditions. Over the years, I learned to listen to my body more on how to take better care of my body by choosing foods that make my body comfortable. Not only is what you eat important but exercise as well, which has always been a part of my life. I grew up playing soccer and today I enjoy swimming, biking, hiking and running on the beach. I can feel all the benefits that my body receives by staying fit and exercising regularly.

There you have it—this is how the five Inner Steps emerged. When you integrate these steps into your life, you begin living with greater clarity, presence, and purpose.

Let's get started.

executing the Inner Steps can make

your dreams a reality

Chapter Five

Execute the Inner Steps

Now that you have the source of inspiration for the Inner Steps, let me guide you in how to incorporate them into your daily life.

Each Inner Step begins with a brief reflection on how the practice has appeared in my own life and how it continues to guide my awareness today. From there, I introduce the step itself and offer practical guidance on how you can begin integrating it into your own daily rhythm.

Each step concludes with a written or reflective exercise designed to help you apply the practice personally. I recommend completing each exercise the first time through, and revisiting them later to observe how your thoughts, feelings, and perspectives may have evolved.

Over time, these steps become less like tasks and more like natural habits of awareness—simple practices that help you reconnect with your inner clarity and the quiet intelligence within.

journaling is like having a trusted friend beside you—
guiding you back to connect to your

Creative Optimum Self

Step One

Journaling

Journaling is a powerful tool that can guide you on this journey today and for years to come. Keeping a journal allows you to safely express the inner voices, desires, and thoughts that arise within your life—gently peeling away the layers that surround the core essence of your soul. Through social conditioning, lack of awareness, and difficult experiences, we all accumulate fears, worries, anxieties, and emotional burdens. Over time, these energies form layers around our true self and begin to influence how we live our lives.

When we are not aware of these layers, our actions are often fueled by them. As a result, we can become unbalanced. If this continues, we may begin to see ourselves through a limited lens—gradually shaping our lives around a limiting story about ourselves. This can lead to feelings of powerlessness, unworthiness, inferiority, and depression. By integrating journaling as a daily practice, you can begin to safely peel away these layers, creating space for greater clarity, balance, and a deeper connection to your inner guide.

How to Begin Journaling

Find a quiet time and place where you can sit with a notebook and be alone with your thoughts. If you can do this in nature or in a harmonious environment, it may deepen the experience—but journaling can be practiced anywhere. Open your notebook and begin writing whatever thoughts, ideas, or inner voices want to be expressed in that moment.

For those who have never kept a journal, beginning may feel uncomfortable or difficult. That is natural. Once you allow yourself to start, the practice can gradually guide you toward positive change. Write everything down—thoughts, fears, worries, insights, and everything in between. This may include what you plan to prepare for dinner, the hope of receiving a call for work, physical discomfort in your body, a phone call you need to make, gratitude for a meal shared with a friend, curiosity about your future, or simply noticing the way trees move in the wind at that moment. The amount of time you write will vary depending on your openness and what is unfolding in your life. One session may take ten minutes; another may take an hour or more.

The most common excuse I hear from clients for not journaling is that they "do not have time." My response is always the same: if writing can help guide positive change in your life, is it not worth a few minutes each day? Even after one session, many people experience a sense of relief. Write until you have nothing more to say. You may notice feeling lighter or more peaceful. Some people cry, some laugh, and others simply grow quiet. This calmer state of mind is closer to who you truly are. As you continue journaling over time, you may become more aware of your thoughts and emotions. When we carry unresolved layers internally, we block our natural state of peace. Often, we are unaware that our current thoughts and actions are being triggered by these layers, which can lead to imbalance. In that state, our actions are often driven by fear, and others can sense it.

When these layers are released safely through writing—and through forgiveness when necessary— relief and healing can occur. You may begin to recognize that you possess an inner wisdom waiting to reconnect with you. This inner wisdom "speaks" through insight, clarity, and guidance. This is your Creative Optimum Self.

Journaling helps cleanse accumulated conditioning and self-doubt and replaces them with awareness. Awareness is the ability to observe the thoughts occupying your mind and recognize that you are aware of them. You become aware of your own awareness. Some people dedicate their entire lives to seeking this state. Some reach it briefly; others never do. In my experience, it requires patience, discipline, and practice. Be gentle with yourself. If journaling is practiced daily—especially when combined with the remaining steps—you may gradually learn to observe your thoughts without becoming them.

Once you become the observer, you begin to realize that you are not your thoughts. They are simply layers accumulated over time. By integrating journaling into your daily life, you can peel away these layers and meet the real you—the silent observer who has lived, lives, and will continue beyond this lifetime's journey. From this place, you gain greater clarity and choice. You may begin replacing habitual thoughts with those that support peace, balance, and fulfillment. When intentions are expressed with clarity and without force, they can align with the larger awareness we all share. This is the universal intelligence—the living awareness that connects us all.

Over time, your Creative Optimum Self may offer insight into why you acted a certain way, reveal solutions to problems, and illuminate the next appropriate step in your life. I would like to share a poem I wrote many years ago, during a period when journaling once again became part of my daily practice after a long absence. One morning session revealed the following:

Find Me

When I am tired, I find me in a swamp.

I strain as I try to feel air.

I strain as I try to touch the passage of time.

I strain as I try to see the light glow over the horizon.

I strain as I try to hear the stars embark on their journey from heaven.

I strain because I find myself in a swamp.

My limbs are locked in chains from fatigue and sleepless nights.

I sink lower in the dark swamp, drowning, taking with me the breath of my youthful seed.

Ultimately, I reach the end of the dreadful swamp and hear a thump in my head.

I find myself at the pit of my mind.

There lies the swamp.

I hear a laugh.

I see a smile.

I feel the warmth of a mother's womb.

My spirit watches me from the stars of tomorrow, wondering why I neglected to grasp the rope of possibility.

I saw no rope to save my body.

Spirit smiles and tells me to open my eyes.

Only then do I see the moment.

I could not see where I was until I found myself hopelessly within the dungeon of my mind.

As spirit spreads the wings of yesterday to return to the bright lights of the future,

I hear a thump in my heart and a whisper as soft as silk:

I am with you.

Find me.

"Find me" is a phrase many hear at some point in their lives—often during moments of difficulty or transition—when they are not living from their soul. It is an invitation from inner wisdom to reconnect. Those who accept this invitation and do the inner work often rediscover their soul as a guide for transformation.

A personal story: while on vacation alone in Antigua, I spent an evening on the beach under the stars, writing in my journal about the kind of partner I hoped to meet—her qualities, values, and presence. I wrote in detail. One month later, on February 14, while exercising in the health club of my residence in New York City, a woman walked in and immediately met my gaze. In that instant, I recognized her as the person I had described in my journal. Yes, I met my former wife on Valentine's night—and it began with writing.

Integrating journaling as a daily practice can be a powerful way to guide, navigate, balance, and reconnect with your Creative Optimum Self.

Recap

1. Set aside time each morning and evening to write in your private journal. A notebook and longhand writing are recommended at first. Begin with twenty minutes and allow flexibility. Find a quiet place where you will not be disturbed—nature if possible.

2. In the morning, write about how you feel, any dreams you remember, and the thoughts or worries that surface. Do not judge them. Simply observe. When your writing settles into a calmer state, you may begin outlining your day or visualizing how you would like it to unfold.

3. In the evening, reflect on your day. Chronicle events as if you were watching the day unfold as a film. Observe moments of challenge, growth, or insight. This practice often brings clarity and supports more peaceful sleep.

4. Keep your journal private. You may share reflections with a deeply trusted, non-judgmental person, but protect the journal itself. It is a personal sanctuary.

Over time, your writing may become less legible as thoughts move quickly. This is normal and often reflects a deeper state of awareness.

Exercise

COS, why?

Answer the following questions quickly in your journal, without overthinking. Write freely.

1. I wish I was _______________________________

Why? _______________________________________

2. I love to _________________________________

Why? _______________________________________

3. I hope to _________________________________

Why? _______________________________________

4. One day, I may ____________________________

Why? _______________________________________

5. I know that ___________________________________

Why?____

6. I believe in __________________________________

Why?____

7. I see beauty in _______________________________

Why? ____

8. I feel anxious when ___________________________

Why? ____

9. I feel relaxed when ___________________________

Why? ____

10. I am ____

Why? ____

Observe your thoughts and allow the writing to guide
you deeper. Over time, journaling may reveal patterns,

uncover blocks, and support self-awareness and growth.

As this practice becomes integrated into your life, you may feel naturally drawn to the next step—meditation.

This exercise awakens awareness—the capacity to observe yourself without judgment.

As you write, ask yourself:

What is my Creative Optimum Self already aware of here that my everyday self may be overlooking?

meditation unleashes your imagination—
you can see, feel, and hear beautiful things
with your eyes closed

Step Two

Meditation

Meditation is the next step in reconnecting with your Creative Optimum Self and supporting meaningful change in your life.

There are many excellent books and techniques that explore meditation. When I first began practicing, I did not know when or how to meditate. Over time—through my own experience and confirmation from my clients—I discovered that journaling first helps prepare the mind for meditation. Journaling clears the surface noise of thoughts and emotions, allowing the mind to arrive at a quieter, more receptive state. As these layers begin to unravel, stillness naturally emerges during meditation. This stillness allows you to hear your innate wisdom.

After journaling, close your eyes and bring your attention to your breath. Simply observe the breath move in and out. At first, your mind may continue to wander—replaying conversations, responsibilities, worries, or hopes. This is completely normal. When I first started meditating, my mind was filled with thoughts like: *What am I doing sitting here? I need to make a phone call. I forgot to pay a bill. I hope someone calls tonight.*

Like many people, I assumed this constant mental activity was simply who I was. After all, we are raised to be thinkers. Many wise teachers have said that true knowledge begins when we can observe our own thoughts. It took time for me to truly understand this. The realization often takes time, but once recognized, it reveals something simple and profound: those thoughts are not who you are. As the mental noise quiets, even briefly, you may experience inner stillness—a meditative state. This is not something you create; it is something you allow. This is your inner wisdom.

For this reason, meditating after journaling can be so effective. Journaling clears the surface, and meditation allows you to rest in silence. From this place, you may begin to sense yourself as more than your physical body—connected to something larger, expansive, and timeless. You are a spiritual being first—a conscious presence whose source is shared with all life. Interestingly, modern science echoes this insight. We now know that everything in the universe—including our bodies—is made of the same fundamental particles, and that most of what we call "matter" is actually empty space filled with potential. Although the Earth travels through space at extraordinary speed, our eyes cannot perceive this movement. There are realities that are true even when we cannot see them.

Consider this: as objects move faster, they become harder to observe in detail. At extreme speeds, they become almost invisible. Light itself travels at extraordinary speed—far beyond the capacity of our senses. At this level, distinctions dissolve. Energy is shared. Separation fades. From this perspective, life takes on a different meaning. We are not isolated beings—we are expressions of the same underlying intelligence. This understanding forms the foundation of Integrated Being Intelligence—the lived integration of awareness, body, mind, relationships, and the world as a unified experience.

Meditation allows you to reconnect with this knowing—not intellectually, but experientially. By visualizing this connection during meditation, you support your ability to remember who you truly are. Life can be hectic and distracting. Meditation brings you back into alignment, grounding you in awareness.

Recap

1. Meditate daily after journaling—in the morning, evening, or whenever you feel disconnected. Set aside ten to fifteen minutes in a quiet, comfortable place.

2. Close your eyes and focus on your breathing. As thoughts arise, let them pass without engagement. If the mind feels restless, return to journaling briefly or use soft music or incense to support stillness.

3. As the breath becomes steady and the mind quieter, imagine yourself as more than the physical body—connected to the air, sky, trees, and all of nature. Sense yourself as part of a larger whole. You are safe.

4. Imagine yourself as a gentle beam of light. Allow that light to fill your body and the space around you. Extend it to your home, your city, the people you encounter, and the places you visit. Let this be an offering of presence and goodwill.

5. Visualize the remainder of your day—where you will go, whom you will meet, what you will do. Bring clarity, focus, and calm awareness into each moment. Move through your day with gratitude and intention.

6. Slowly open your eyes. Stay alert, aware, and connected to your Creative Optimum Self as you continue your day.

Exercise

There are two ways you can deepen your meditation practice:

1.   Guided Mantra Practice

Many meditation books offer valuable guidance. One of my favorites is *Spontaneous Fulfillment of Desire* by Deepak Chopra, particularly the chapter on meditation and mantras. Chopra introduces sutras—ancient intentions designed to take awareness deeper.

One such sutra is:

Aham Brahmasmi

I am the ripple in the fabric of the cosmos.

The core of my being is the ultimate reality, the root and ground of the universe, the source of all that exists.

Imagine that the whole universe is being played out inside of me.

Imagine that I am connected to everything that exists.

Imagine that I am like a crystal bead. I reflect the light of all other sentient beings. I also reflect the light of the whole universe.

Imagine that I am a strand in the cosmic thread connected to all the other strands.

Imagine that I am eternal.

2. Create Your Own Meditation

Use the recap above as a foundation. Add instrumental music or natural sounds—ocean waves, rain, or forest air. After meditation, write or reflect on the following statements:

I am awake and alert.

I release fear, worry, and tension.

My body is a vessel for awareness.

I am connected with life.

I trust the wisdom within me.

I move with clarity and purpose.

I am love. I am presence.

We are connected.

Over time, these reflections may evolve naturally as your awareness deepens. Allow the practice to grow with you.

This exercise cultivates presence—the ability to rest in awareness without effort or striving.

As you meditate, ask yourself:

What becomes visible when I stop trying to observe and simply allow awareness to observe itself?

*inspirational reading touches your soul and
stirs your imagination*

Step Three

Inspirational Reading

Inspirational reading is a powerful companion on this journey.

Today there are millions of publications and books available, along with thousands of hours of television, advertisements, and digital media filling our daily lives. Information appears everywhere—in subways, on buses, on billboards, across screens, and devices. Everywhere we turn, something competes for our attention. The internet, email, social media, and now artificial intelligence deliver an endless stream of information. Even with sophisticated filtering tools, we still absorb far more than the mind is designed to process. Much of this information consumes time, fragments attention, and creates mental clutter. It can feel as if the entire world is competing for our focus. When the mind is constantly cluttered, we forget who we are and fall into the belief that we must absorb and react to everything. This disconnects us from our soul. By consciously selecting reading material that is inspirational to the mind and spirit, you can remain connected to your Creative Optimum Self.

Many poets, writers, philosophers, and scientists have created work that awakens something deep within us. The subject matter itself matters less than the effect it has on the reader. What matters is that the reading genuinely inspires, stirs something within, and reconnects us to our inner guide. Personally, I am inspired by writers such as Julia Cameron, Emmet Fox, and Og Mandino among others. I still remember the first time I read *The Prophet.* I was deeply moved by its timeless wisdom and simplicity. Inspirational reading may awaken the desire to write, to paint, to reach out to a friend, or to explore something new.

When reading touches the soul, it activates creativity and awareness. To be inspired at this level is to live a more loving, inspiring, and fulfilling existence.

I encourage you to incorporate inspirational reading into your daily life—even for a few minutes a day. This can be during your morning journaling and meditation, while commuting, after a meal, or during any pause in your routine. Inspirational reading does not require long periods of time—only intention. One book that has been part of my morning ritual is *Heart Steps: Prayers and Declarations for a Creative Life* by Julia Cameron. Each page offers a short reflection followed by a prayer or declaration that invites stillness and awareness.

One passage includes the following reflection:

The universe responds to my dreams and needs.

There is a unity flowing through all things.

*We are co-creative beings working with—and within—
a larger whole.*

*Drawing upon this inner source, we have an unlimited
supply.*

When you read passages like this, allow yourself to
reflect and write about what they awaken within you.
Inspirational reading, combined with journaling and
meditation, deepens your connection to your
Integrated Being Intelligence—the intelligence of an
aware, integrated, and present being.

Although we appear different on the surface—with
unique goals, careers, and ambitions—at the soul level,
we want the same things. We seek expression,
connection, appreciation, and fulfillment. Each of us
carries a story, and every story ultimately moves
toward the same destination. We may walk different
paths, but we emerge from the same source.

Recap

1. During or after meditation, select a prayer, passage, or inspirational reading—about five minutes—from a trusted source.

2. Notice how you feel after reading and write freely in your journal. Explore what the passage evokes and how it relates to your life. Even familiar words can reveal new insight when revisited.

3. Carry inspirational readings with you. When you feel disconnected, overwhelmed, or mentally scattered, pause and read for a few minutes to reconnect with your inner guide.

Exercise

Return to the passage above and answer the following questions in your journal. There are no right or wrong answers. Write freely and allow the process to guide you.

1. Am I aware of the power behind the words I use each day?

2. Do I choose my words consciously or speak out of habit?

3. Do I believe the universe hears my intentions and desires? When was the last time I experienced this?

4. What is my personal definition of the universe? Unity?

5. What is Source, and how do I remain connected to it?

Keep your responses in your journal. Revisit these questions after completing this book and integrating the ten steps into your daily life. Observe how your answers evolve as your awareness deepens.

This exercise awakens discernment—the capacity to recognize how intention, language, and belief shape lived reality.

As you reflect, ask yourself:

What am I already creating through my words and definitions?

nature and solitude bring you
closer to heaven on earth

Step Four

Nature and Solitude

Nature, at its source, is innocent and whole—free from ego as humans experience it. The sun shines, trees grow, water flows, rain falls, birds fly—all of nature follows its own rhythm and lives as it was created to live. Nature and solitude are the next steps in living from the Creative Optimum Self.

The elements of nature do not concern themselves with judgment or comparison. The sun does not worry whether the moon will appear at night. The sun and the moon trust the unseen intelligence of the universe— that everything will unfold in harmony, that rising and setting will occur as they always have. The same is true of all natural elements. They have not developed the human ego or the perception of doubt. Nature is connected to the soul of the universe and exists in peace, harmony, and love. It is a living expression of infinite integrated intelligence, offering its wisdom simply by being.

As humans, we can learn from nature by observing how effortlessly it lives. Make it a priority to spend time in nature. This can be a walk in the park, a run along the ocean, a hike in the mountains, gazing at a forest, or sitting quietly by a lake. Observe how nature allows all forms to exist exactly as they are meant to be. There is harmony, grace, and connection everywhere.

When you feel inspired by nature, it is because you recognize something of yourself within it. Although the ocean does not physically resemble us, we connect to it because we are made of the same underlying elements and share the same source of life. It is this connection that allows inspiration to arise. Spending time in nature restores a sense of safety and belonging. It calms the nervous system and allows your soul to reconnect with the universal source. In this space, you can hear your inner voice—your guide—and access creativity with greater ease.

The second part of this step is spending time alone. Time alone may be twenty minutes, a few hours, a day, or longer. Modern life can be overwhelming, filled with responsibilities, endless stimulation, and constant engagement. Without intentional pauses, it becomes easy to lose focus and disconnect from inner wisdom. Some people find solitude challenging. Often, this is because constant stimulation is used to avoid facing thoughts, emotions, or unresolved experiences. By staying busy with external distractions, there is no space to listen inwardly. This pattern blocks access to the inner guide.

When issues remain unaddressed, they create energetic clutter and drain vitality. Choosing not to face inner truths does not only affect the individual— it contributes to disorder in the larger system. We are all connected, and internal chaos disrupts universal flow. Spending time alone allows you to recharge, regroup, and realign with yourself. In solitude, you reconnect with your soul. By listening inwardly, you gain access to wisdom, creativity, and clarity that cannot be found externally.

By regularly spending time in nature and in solitude, you deepen your relationship with the universe and your soul. As this connection strengthens, access to wisdom, intelligence, and insight becomes more available in the present moment.

Recap

1. Schedule daily time with nature. This may be brief—walking through a park, sitting by a lake, watching birds or waves—or extended, such as hiking, biking, or running outdoors.

2. While in nature, remain fully present. Observe without distraction. This is an ideal time to journal, meditate, or read inspirational material.

3. Recognize that your ability to connect with nature exists because you and nature are made of the same

energy, continuously exchanging it—such as the oxygen you breathe in.

4.   Notice how you feel during and after time in nature. Peace arises naturally. This peace is always accessible and lives in the present moment. It is your inner guide.

5. Schedule regular time alone. This may include journaling, meditation, reading, walking, sightseeing, or simply being with your thoughts. Release external focus and allow attention to return inward. Resistance may arise at first, but over time, solitude becomes nourishing. Within it, you access silence—your Creative Optimum Self.

Exercise

This visualization explores the wisdom revealed through nature and solitude.

Find a quiet, comfortable place, as you would for meditation. Imagine yourself in the middle of the ocean—on a boat, swimming, or resting safely on a floating platform. You see water all around you, with the shoreline visible in the distance. Observe the waves. Each wave is unique—different in size, shape, and rhythm. Yet all waves move together, guided by an unseen current beneath the surface. Notice how the waves travel toward the shore and eventually arrive together. Some arrive with more force, others gently, but all are carried by the same invisible intelligence.

Now reflect on your life. Let the shoreline represent peace, fulfillment, love, and wisdom. Let yourself be one of the waves, moving alongside countless others—each on a unique path, yet guided by the same current. Although paths differ, the destination is shared. This invisible force—the soul—keeps all movement aligned.

By staying connected to your Creative Optimum Self, you navigate life with harmony and reach your destination with clarity and grace.

This exercise awakens trust—the capacity to move with life without needing to control every outcome.

As you reflect, ask yourself:

Where in my life am I resisting the current instead of allowing my Creative Optimum Self to guide the movement?

well-being makes you a shining star

Step Five

Well-Being

As you integrate journaling, meditation, inspirational reading, and time in nature and solitude into a daily practice, you naturally become more aware of how you feel—physically, emotionally, and energetically—in relation to yourself and the world around you. Your senses sharpen as you observe your thoughts and gently peel away layers formed through conditioning and experience. As this awareness deepens, kindness toward yourself becomes essential. Forgiveness—of yourself and others—allows space for renewal. The past no longer defines you. The present moment is always available, and every moment offers a new beginning. That beginning starts with how you care for yourself and your overall well-being.

Well-being is not a destination; it is a daily relationship. Taking care of your body through mindful nourishment, movement, rest, and stress awareness supports your connection to Integrated Being Intelligence—the wisdom that unifies body, mind, and soul. The body is a precious and intelligent vessel that functions with extraordinary complexity on its own. Cells digest food, repair tissue, regulate systems, and protect you continuously without conscious effort. Your responsibility is not to control the body—it is to treat it kindly.

Challenges arise when this responsibility is neglected. Because we have choice in how we eat, drink, move, and live, those choices directly affect how the body performs. When awareness is absent, imbalance can arise—often expressed through excess, addiction, or disregard for the body's signals. At the core of many unhealthy patterns is a temporary loss of self-respect. Yet at any moment, a new choice can be made. When conscious choices replace unconscious ones, the body responds with resilience and healing. This is one of its great gifts.

Cultural conditioning often shapes our eating habits. Growing up in an Italian family, food was central to daily life—preparation, sharing, celebration. While this brought connection and joy, it also encouraged overeating beyond what the body needed. Over time, I shifted from "living to eat" to eating to live optimally— listening to what the body actually requires rather than what tradition or habit dictates. The body provides clear signals when we learn to listen. It thrives on fresh water. It thrives on nutrients found in fruits, vegetables, legumes, and whole foods. It also requires proteins and healthy fats sourced from plants or animals depending on individual needs.

Because the body expends more energy while awake, it benefits from nourishment earlier in the day and lighter intake before rest. There is no universal diet. Genetics, upbringing, and lifestyle all influence what supports optimal well-being. While many experts offer guidance, your body is the ultimate authority.

Keeping a food journal—noting what you eat, how much, and how you feel afterward—creates awareness that no external plan can replace. The body speaks through sensation, energy, clarity, and discomfort. For example, certain foods may create lethargy or mental fog, while others support alertness and vitality. When you notice these patterns, choice becomes natural rather than forced. Eating well supports healthy weight and balance, but enjoyment also matters. Sharing meals should be peaceful and nourishing—not only physically, but emotionally. The environment in which you eat matters. Tension, conflict, or distraction can disrupt digestion just as much as unconscious food choices. You can choose warmth, presence, and gratitude around meals—whether shared with others or enjoyed alone. In doing so, you nourish the body with both food and energy.

Movement is another essential expression of well-being. Always consult a medical professional before beginning any exercise program, but recognize that movement supports vitality, clarity, and emotional balance. Different forms of exercise affect us differently. Team sports foster connection and synchronization. Outdoor activities expand perspective. Swimming soothes and centers. Each form offers unique feedback. Journaling after movement helps you understand which practices best support your body and mind.

Rest and sleep are equally vital to maintain balance, clarity, and overall well-being. While recommendations vary, most people thrive with consistent, adequate rest. Observing your body's natural rhythms allows you to understand what works best for you. When the body is rested, clarity increases and anxiety decreases. The body communicates constantly—through energy, discomfort, desire, and intuition. When you listen, a bond forms. This relationship becomes a dialogue rather than a struggle.

The body is not separate from wisdom; it is wisdom in form. By honoring the body's intelligence and responding with awareness, you support its optimal function. When the body functions well, it becomes a stable foundation for connection to your soul, allowing you to live more fully from your Creative Optimum Self.

Recap

1. Recognize the body as intelligent, complex, and wise. It performs countless functions automatically; your role is to support it with conscious choices.

2. Keep a food journal to observe what you eat, how much, and how you feel afterward. Favor fresh, natural foods that support clarity and energy.

3. Use weight and health guidelines as reference points, not rigid rules. Your body will guide you toward its optimal balance.

4. Create a peaceful, attentive environment when eating. Presence enhances nourishment.

5. Engage in regular movement that energizes, relieves stress, and feels enjoyable. Vary activities to maintain enthusiasm.

6. Honor rest and sleep. Observe what restores you best and respond accordingly. Support the body with care when it signals the need for recovery.

Exercise

For one month, use journaling to observe your body's needs.

Each day, record:

1. What you ate and drank, how much, and when.

2. How you felt afterward—physically, emotionally, and mentally.

3. The type and duration of exercise performed.

4. How you felt during and after movement—including thoughts, insights, or creative ideas.

5. When you woke up and how you felt upon waking, including any dreams.

6. When you went to bed and how easily you fell asleep.

This practice deepens awareness of what truly supports your well-being. As your body functions optimally, your connection to your Creative Optimum Self strengthens naturally.

This inner stability becomes the fuel for how you lead, relate, and execute in the world with clarity.

This exercise awakens discernment—the ability to listen to your body's intelligence and respond with clarity rather than habit.

As you reflect, ask yourself:

What is my Creative Optimum Self revealing about how my body wants to be cared for right now?

Transforming your world
is within reach.

PART III

Transform Your World

Before moving forward, it's important to name what is unfolding here.

The Inner Steps you have just completed cultivate awareness, presence, and coherence within. When this inner intelligence is lived consistently, it does not remain contained—it expresses itself outwardly.

What emerges naturally from the Creative Optimum Self—and from the lived awareness of Integrated Being Intelligence—is a way of thinking, relating, deciding, and serving in the world that is grounded, responsible, and effective. This outward expression becomes Integrated Leadership Intelligence—not as a role or title, but as a way of operating in life with clarity, responsibility, and care.

The five Inner Steps will guide you to become more open and aware of everything around you. As you execute these steps regularly and over time, you will begin to see a transformation in your life as this inner awareness becomes more present in how you live. You may notice greater energy, feel and look more vibrant, and become more attuned to your body and the life around you. As you interact with the rest of the world, people will begin to notice a change in you.

This brings us to the five Outer Steps that ensure your transformation continues on this journey. The Outer Steps are: living with no loose ends; nurturing all relationships; being warm and gracious; being passionate and grateful; and living from your Creative Optimum Self as the eyes and ears of the universe.

Together, they translate your inner awareness into lived expression—where Integrated Leadership Intelligence becomes visible in how you think, act, relate, and serve each day. This is where your life begins to influence and elevate the world around you.

Outer Steps are grounded in truth,
honor, and order

Chapter Six

Inspiration for Outer Steps

The Outer Steps are inspired by the years of experience and success I gained in the business world. Business—and any form of work—is part of life. If we can succeed in one part of life, business in this case, we can leverage what we have learned that works and incorporate it into other parts of our lives. The five Outer Steps are based on the five principles that I have used successfully in all my work with companies, clients, and family business.

From delivering espresso at five years old to delivering Creative Optimum Services to Wall Street firms, the projects and the people may change but the principles for success remain the same. I have worked with people from all professions and walks of life, across many industries and all levels of management. During my career, I have worked on a wide range of projects—from complex, high-profile, multi-billion dollar initiatives to smaller, one month projects. I have come to master the five principles—or keys—that support success in any type of work. The five principles are efficiency, relationships, flexible process, leadership, and creativity.

Over time, I came to see that success—whether personal or professional—is not accidental. It follows a clear framework. Through this framework, I have successfully executed a wide range of projects and initiatives. As a result, clients have benefited through reduced costs, increased productivity, and stronger sales and profits. When I expanded my consulting practice and included personal transformation workshops, I turned to these same principles for guidance in developing five Outer Steps for personal and social transformation. I leveraged what works in one part of life to assist in transforming another part of life.

Each of the five Outer Steps is derived from and related to the five business principles. When you live with no loose ends, you have order in your life, less clutter in your mind and in your environment. There is efficiency. The next outer step is to nurture all relationships which is the same as developing and maintaining solid business relationships. Thirdly, be warm and gracious implies that you are respectful and flexible with all your worldly interactions. The next outer step is to be passionate and grateful which are also two key qualities of a successful business leader. And the final outer step is to live from your Creative Optimum Self which is the lived expression of Integrated Leadership Intelligence.

Let's begin executing the Outer Steps.

*executing the Outer Steps aligns you
with the manifestation of
universal dreams*

Chapter Seven

Execute the Outer Steps

Now that you have the inspiration behind the Outer Steps, let me guide you in how to incorporate them into your daily life.

Just as you learned to integrate the Inner Steps through awareness and repetition, the Outer Steps require the same steady application—this time expressed in how you relate, decide, and serve in the world. These steps translate inner awareness into practical action, shaping the way you conduct yourself in everyday situations and interactions.

Each step concludes with a written or visual exercise. I recommend completing each exercise the first time through, then revisiting them periodically to observe and compare how your results evolve over time.

live with no loose ends, and
life flows freely

Step Six

Live with No Loose Ends

As you integrate the Inner Steps into your daily life, you become more connected with your inner guide and more comfortable in your own skin. You grow more aware, more curious, and more receptive to learning from your experiences. This curiosity naturally draws you into deeper interaction with the world—which leads naturally to the first outer step: living with no loose ends.

Living with no loose ends is a powerful way to access your inner wisdom because there is less mental clutter blocking the flow. I define a loose end this way: when you intentionally think, say, or write that you will do something positive, and then do not follow through. Many people live this way without realizing the cost. Over time, this pattern creates stress, anxiety, strained relationships, and inefficiencies—not only for the individual, but for everyone they interact with.

If you carry a loose end in your mind—a phone call you meant to make, a bill you intended to pay, an appointment you never scheduled, a creative project you postponed—your attention is fragmented. When your attention is fragmented, you are not fully present. When you are not present, you miss life as it unfolds. When presence is compromised, joy diminishes. Peace becomes harder to access. Clarity fades. When we engage with others from this state, we unconsciously transmit confusion, stress, and impatience. The world absorbs that energy. Yet the opposite is also true. When we live with no loose ends, the world benefits. Just as journaling clears inner clutter, this outer step supports that inner clarity while bringing your intentions into completion—releasing that energy into the world with integrity, trust, and positive impact.

A simple example illustrates this well. Imagine you secure a hard-to-get reservation at a popular restaurant on Valentine's Day. The host asks that you please call if you need to cancel, as there is a long waiting list. Your plans change, and you decide not to go—but you forget to call. The restaurant is left with an empty table. The staff earns less that evening. And somewhere on that waiting list is a couple hoping to celebrate a meaningful anniversary who never gets the call. One unclosed loop creates a ripple of consequence. When we follow through, harmony is restored. While the universe—with its unseen intelligence—often works to correct imbalance, we are still responsible for doing our part. There is order in life. When we intend to do something positive and do not follow through, we introduce disorder. And the larger intelligence must compensate to realign the system.

Here is another example. I once met someone at a health club and felt an immediate connection. We spoke about going on a bike ride together, and I told him I would email to set it up. Days passed, and I did not follow through. Each time I returned to the club, I ran into him—and each time I was reminded of my loose end. It felt as though life itself was nudging me forward, signaling that this connection mattered. Eventually, I followed through. We went on that ride, and I discovered he was a senior leader at a financial firm I had long hoped to work with. That one act of completion led to a meaningful friendship and a professional engagement.

Loose ends block opportunity. Completion opens doors. Writing this book was, for a long time, my biggest loose end. I spoke about it for years. People encouraged me. I planned, brainstormed, and delayed. Until one day my former wife looked at me and said, "You're teaching people to live with no loose ends—yet this book is your biggest one." Not long after, several major business deals unexpectedly fell through. Suddenly, time and space appeared. The moment I began writing, I could not stop. The unseen intelligence orchestrated the conditions—but only after I was finally ready to follow through.

Today, technology makes living with no loose ends easier than ever. Calendars, reminders, messaging, and mobile devices allow us to close loops quickly and efficiently. When we complete what we begin, we create mental spaciousness. The mind becomes an open vessel—ready to receive insight, creativity, and inspiration. This inspiration is always present. Living with no loose ends allows us to meet it fully.

Recap

1. Make a daily list of tasks you intend to complete. Prioritize them and cross them off as they are completed.

2. Review your list each day and distinguish between daily actions and long-term goals. Long-term goals belong on a separate project list.

3. Record in your journal how you feel when items are completed—and how you feel when they are not. This awareness strengthens your connection to inner wisdom.

Exercise

Make a complete list of everything you have said you would do or complete—bills, calls, projects, goals, ideas.

Assign each item a realistic completion date. Keep this list visible and update it daily.

As you practice this, observe how clarity, energy, and creativity increase.

This exercise awakens integrity—the coherence between what you say, what you choose, and what you complete.

As you review your list, ask yourself:

Where is my Creative Optimum Self already clear, and where am I being invited to bring my actions into greater alignment?

nurturing all relationships can cleanse
and rejuvenate your soul

Step Seven

Nurture All Relationships

As you begin incorporating living with no loose ends into your daily life, you become more connected with your inner guide. You grow more aware of who you truly are, more curious about the world around you, and more attuned to the universe. You begin to see—not as an idea, but as a lived truth—that your thoughts, words, and actions impact your life, the people around you, and the world at large. With greater clarity in your life, more order in your mind and home, and more energy to share, your transformation deepens through a powerful realization: the value of your relationships. As you follow through consistently, the people around you begin to trust you more, and your relationships naturally deepen.

This brings us to the next outer step—nurture all relationships. As you respect, love, and practice honesty within your relationships, you learn more about yourself and the people around you, and you naturally become a guide for others as they reconnect with their own inner awareness. By living this way, you experience—directly—how deeply connected we are to one another. If you choose to be open and nurture your relationships, others are influenced by your example. Living with respect, love, and truth asks very little—yet the return is priceless. You feel lighter.

Warmer inside. It feels natural—like the sun shining without asking permission.

Nurture all relationships: the relationship you have with yourself; your family; friends; adversaries; community; government; foreigners; business colleagues; the environment; nature—and even those whose actions cause harm in the world. Many people struggle with the idea of extending respect toward someone who has caused suffering. But remember: even though we appear and behave differently, at the soul level we come from the same Source. This does not excuse wrongdoing. It does not remove accountability. It points to something deeper: a person can lose connection to their inner goodness for a time, and still possess a soul capable of reconnection—and our approach to healing the world must include wisdom, not punishment alone.

We have already discussed nurturing yourself through well-being—eating consciously, exercising, and resting. Some people call this selfish. It is not. It is a form of responsibility. If you wish to be a guiding light and a stabilizing presence for others, your energy must first be rooted, clear, and strong. When you nurture your body and mind and keep your vessel healthy, you become capable of offering goodness, love, and harmony without depletion. It took me a long time to understand this. Growing up, I naturally assumed the role of caretaker. I focused on solving other people's problems, fixing what was broken, and restoring harmony. I often intervened when my parents argued. I would try to protect others from discomfort and stress. While it felt meaningful to help, I often had little energy left for myself. Today, I still assist others—but I do it from a stronger self. I know who I am first. I take care of my needs, and as a result, my intentions come from a deeper truth. My energy is stronger, more stable, and more healing.

Family

Nurturing your family is one of the most powerful teachers on this journey. Over time, if you stay connected, you begin to see your parents not only as parents, but as human beings—people with dreams, fears, regrets, anxieties, and a soul. Their soul comes from the same Source as yours. When you view your family at this level, compassion becomes possible— even when you disagree, even when you witness behavior that is not right.

Growing up, I was close with both of my parents, but my relationship with each was different. I looked up to my father and learned a great deal of business and life wisdom from him. But I also observed that he had a temper and a short fuse. Although I was never physically abused by my father, the same could not be said for my mother and brother. When I witnessed these events, I intervened. I stopped what I could. I worked to restore peace. I could see that my father loved my mother and his elder son deeply—yet at times he could not control his anger. He did not know how to handle stress, and he expressed it in harmful ways. When I was young, I did not feel strong enough to confront him. When my parents argued, I often stepped in simply to separate them, but the issue itself was never openly discussed.

The situation continued for years. Then one day, when I was sixteen, something in me reached its limit. I found the courage to confront him physically and pinned him against the wall. In that moment, something shifted. The abuse stopped after that confrontation. Before he died at the young age of fifty-seven, he reconciled his differences with my mother and brother. But reconciliation came at a cost. If we had addressed the issue earlier—clearly, honestly, and courageously— we might have shared more loving years without carrying such expensive baggage.

My relationship with my mother was more wholesome. Growing up, I learned wisdom from her that I still live by. She is one of the most courageous people I have ever known. After I graduated high school, our relationship began to shift. I became more independent and relied less on her guidance. As a mother, she struggled with that change. After my father died, she became depressed and very ill, and the roles reversed. I became the caretaker. Over time she regained much of her independence and health— running on the beach and swimming in the pool. It was a joy to see her live again, and she credits my support and the same ten steps described in this book for guiding her back to her inner wisdom. Eventually, she did lose her independence and relied on mobility support and help at home. She often complained of pain that doctors could not fully diagnose. Still, I provided support, love, and respect—and I also spoke truthfully about my concerns because real love includes honesty.

Sometimes you may need to go separate ways—but true love can still return. My brother and I were very close growing up. He was my best friend. But as we got older, especially in my twenties, friction entered the relationship. In part, it was because I was no longer his "little brother." I needed him differently, and he still wanted to protect and manage things for me. After he married, we grew apart. Even then, at the soul level, we loved each other. When I saw him in a toxic marriage, I supported him and told him the truth. At the time, he could not accept it, and we went without a relationship for a long period. I always offered him unconditional love, supported him during his divorce, and later supported him as he found new love and family.

Intimate relationships

An intimate relationship will evolve over time as two people grow—individually and together. What matters most is the foundation: respect, honesty, and the willingness to learn. It does not take much effort to be kind to the people you love—yet kindness is often the first thing people forget. You will not agree on everything. But if you seek to understand why your partner feels as they do, and if you offer respect as a human being first, you can create a healthy relationship. Sometimes it becomes clear that you are no longer capable of living together in harmony. If compromise is not possible and suffering becomes the norm, it may be wiser to go separate ways—respectfully, compassionately, and truthfully—because truth reconnects you with your inner guide. And from that place, the right next step becomes clearer.

Children

When you extend unconditional love to children—whether they are part of your family or not—you will witness innate wisdom. Children are born innocent and pure, relatively clean of labels and judgments. They need guidance, support, and a loving environment to mature into emotionally healthy human beings. Some people forget this and treat children with little respect, as if they are not wise enough, smart enough, or worthy of being heard. In some situations, this becomes far worse—adults resort to emotional or physical harm to enforce control.

When children experience this kind of suffering, they accumulate layers of fear, anger, and low self-worth around their soul as they grow. Many spend adulthood trying to remove these layers and reclaim their real self. Others repeat the pattern and pass suffering forward. This cycle can change. It begins when children are nurtured with love, respect, and stability so they can mature with confidence and inner peace. I can relate to this journey, having had to gently peel away my own layers over time to reconnect with who I truly am.

Friends and adversaries

When you bring respect, compassion, and honesty to your friends, you gain wisdom and become a source of inspiration. Friendships vary—deep bonds, distant friendships, lifelong friends you rarely see, and friends with whom you share only certain seasons of life. Regardless of distance or frequency, you can still connect with their soul. Celebrate your friends and their differences. When you share time together—in person, by phone, or through social media—be honorable and respectful. A warm feeling rises within you because you are touching your own soul in another form. And from that place, "magic moments" are real.

Even your adversaries deserve respect. An adversary is often a label created by ego and social conditioning—someone who holds different political, religious, business, or personal beliefs. But beliefs change. Friends can become adversaries. Adversaries can become friends. If you treat people with dignity, you create the conditions for learning, resolution, and sometimes transformation.

Even those who commit great harm in the world can benefit from understanding—not as permission, but as part of a deeper solution. You may ask: how can we respect someone who has taken life or committed brutal harm? There is no tolerance for these acts, and appropriate action must be taken. Yet purely punitive systems have not eliminated violence. A more enduring approach requires understanding why people become capable of violence—the patterns of upbringing, trauma, despair, and disconnection. The soul was not born harmful. Something went wrong. And while accountability is necessary, it is also true that humans can transform.

As we grow in awareness and live from our Creative Optimum Self, we become beings who respect life, love deeply, and live truthfully. If transformation is possible for one, it is possible for many—and building a better world requires practical programs that nurture this transformation early, including in schools and workplaces. It may take time, but it is worth the journey.

Community, daily life, work, and travel

In your community, be conscious of needs. Volunteer. Open the door for someone. Help the elderly with groceries. Smile with your eyes. Greet people by name. Say please and thank you. The energy you give becomes the atmosphere you live in. Some people believe that paying for a service gives them permission to be disrespectful. Money does not create inner richness or dignity. In fact, living unkindly is a form of poverty—because it separates you from your own soul. Be kind to your waitress, your bus driver, your banker. When someone thanks you, consider "You're welcome," or "My pleasure," rather than "No problem." Often "no problem" is harmless habit—but when used unconsciously it can imply there was a problem to begin with. Words matter. They either unify or separate.

When you travel, be curious and respectful. Don't assume others speak your language. Remember the power of the unspoken gesture. Appreciate new foods, new customs, new landscapes. Show kindness and you will often feel embraced—because when you live from soul, you feel at home wherever you are.

At work, live from the same place. Some people think they must become a different person professionally— hide feelings, avoid truth, and suppress authenticity. This creates inefficiencies and mistrust. Bring your soul to work. It creates harmony, invites honest communication, and makes space for great ideas.

Truth and respect are not weaknesses in business—they are the foundation of real excellence. Integrity builds trust, and trust is the unseen structure that allows leadership to function without force.

Government and environment

Nurture your relationship with your government by showing respect, being truthful about needs, and participating in civic life. When people disengage, leadership becomes disconnected from the lived needs of the majority. Engagement—expressed with intelligence and integrity—is part of responsible citizenship.

Nurture your environment. Clean up after yourself in public spaces. Refrain from littering. Put things back. When you create disorder, you create work for someone else. Be conscious of how you live inside and outside your home. Make choices that create harmony, safety, and order—because the environment is not "outside" you. It is part of you.

Nature and Bianco

Nature teaches presence. Nature also teaches rhythm and patience. Nothing blooms out of season. The soil must be prepared, the seed planted, the roots strengthened before growth becomes visible. When we rush what requires cultivation, we create strain;

when we honor the process, life unfolds with quiet intelligence.

If we are open, we can be surprised by the teachers that appear along the way. A beautiful Pekingese dog named Bianco taught me the meaning of living in the moment. Bianco was an old soul. Every morning, he would go into our garden and smell every flower, branch, and leaf as though he was encountering it for the first time. Watching him, I realized how beautiful his world was—and how fully alive he was inside it. That is living in the moment—without labels, judgments, or stale assumptions. When you live this way, you learn. You become inspired. And you rediscover joy.

From here, warmth and graciousness stop being an effort—they become your natural expression.

Recap

1. Nurturing all relationships begins with yourself. By nurturing your health and inner life, you build the stability needed to nurture others without depletion.

2. Extend love and understanding to your family. With time, truth, and compassion, you can become a source of inspiration for transformation.

3.   Express unconditional love to your loved ones and to children. A harmonious environment allows souls to mature without unnecessary layers of fear and anger.

4.   Nurture friends and adversaries with respect. You may not connect with everyone the same way, but you can learn from all, and sometimes adversaries become allies.

5.   It takes maturity to understand that even those deeply disconnected can transform. Accountability is necessary—and wisdom requires understanding the deeper causes.

6.   Nurture community: neighbors, strangers, service professionals, and daily interactions. Living soul-to-soul elevates the world.

7. Nurture nature and environment. Make daily choices that support cleanliness, safety, and harmony. Nature rewards curiosity and teaches presence—and presence reconnects you to your deeper awareness.

Exercise

1. In your journal, list your relationship groups: yourself, family, friends, adversaries, business colleagues, community, service professionals, foreigners, environment, nature.

2. For each group, list names (and for community include neighbors, doorman, drivers, and a subgroup: strangers). Under environment include public spaces you use.

3. For each name, write one simple, practical action that expresses respect, kindness, honesty, or understanding.

4. Put it into practice. For those you won't see soon, visualize your action during meditation.

5. Observe what happens. Everyone wants to be understood, respected, and loved. It costs little—and it changes everything.

With commitment, we can graciously transform the world.

This exercise awakens relational awareness—the capacity to lead with presence, dignity, and discernment in every interaction.

As you observe what unfolds, ask yourself:

How is my Creative Optimum Self already shaping my relationships—and where is it inviting me to lead with greater clarity, compassion, or courage?

be warm and gracious—
your presence warms
the world around you

Step Eight

Be Warm and Gracious

As you appreciate and nurture all your relationships, you begin to understand that your existence matters—and that your thoughts, words, and actions shape the world around you. At this point, you recognize that living from your Creative Optimum Self is the only way to live fully—because at this level, worries and anxieties naturally diminish. You may still experience moments of doubt or weakness, but you now handle them differently—you respond from strength rather than fear.

This strength comes from your soul—eternal, abundant, and always available when you choose to align with it. You recognize that this soul is not separate from others. It is part of the same universal intelligence that flows through all life. You feel lighter. Your presence becomes calming and reassuring. People notice you—not because you seek attention, but because warmth radiates from you naturally. Your words carry kindness, your actions are gracious, and your energy invites trust.

All the steps you have practiced thus far have transformed you into a warm and gracious being. This quality was always within you; it was simply hidden beneath layers of fear, conditioning, and distraction.

Now, you are awake. You are aware not only of what you see with your physical eyes, but also of what you sense inwardly. You understand that some experiences cannot be explained logically—only felt. You think of relocating, and suddenly signs of that place appear everywhere. You consider a vacation, and an unexpected invitation arrives. You worry about finances, and an unforeseen opportunity presents itself. These are not random—they are engineered by the universal Source when you align gracefully with life.

Living warmly and graciously places you in harmony with the flow of the universe. When you embody this state, compassion becomes effortless. You are approachable, genuine, and present. People feel safe with you because they sense truth—not performance—in your being. Some may feel inspired. Others may feel intimidated, unsure if they can live this way themselves. But as you connect with them at the soul level, they begin to remember that this grace exists within them too. With this presence, you naturally diffuse conflict. Tension softens in your presence. Even unresolved disagreements begin to move toward understanding. Your energy encourages reason, civility, and compromise—often without a single word spoken.

This is transformation at its purest—bringing light into darkness without needing recognition. As you share your love and grace with the world, you attract others who live from the same place. Communities form. Ideas flow. Solutions emerge. Harmony expands. Together, people bonded by this energy accomplish what once felt impossible.

In this unity, you gain a deeper understanding of existence itself. You see clearly that life responds to the choices you make. When your choices are grounded in love, truth, and harmony, life responds with opportunity, protection, and guidance. This wisdom lives in the moment. Some are disconnected from it temporarily; others may lose alignment with it for a time. But truth and order always prevail. Energy returns to its source. What is given comes back—in time.

By living warmly and graciously, you become part of Integrated Being Intelligence—the Creative Optimum Self in action. Together, we generate infinite love and gratitude for LIFE—

Loving, Inspiring, Fulfilling Existence.

Recap

1. Live warmly and graciously in all that you say and do, and peace will follow.

2.   You diffuse conflict and inspire harmony through your presence.

3.   You connect authentically with all beings and bring out their best.

4.   Guided by inner wisdom, you live in the flow of life and inspire others to do the same.

Exercise

This is a visual and transformative exercise.

Find a quiet, comfortable place to sit. Close your eyes. Focus on your breathing, preparing yourself as if you were about to meditate.

Imagine yourself seated in a warm, inviting movie theater on opening night. The audience is excited. Anticipation fills the room.

Choose a movie you love—one with a character admired by all. Watch closely. Notice how they move, speak, and respond. Observe how their presence makes you feel uplifted.

Now imagine yourself stepping into that role. You become the star of the film. Feel the audience respond to your presence. When the movie ends, the applause is genuine. People leave inspired, joyful, and changed.

This exercise reminds you that life unfolds like a film—and you are both the one living the moment and the one shaping how the story moves forward. In every scene, you have the opportunity to choose how you appear, how you respond, and how you treat others.

When you live this way, you naturally inspire others to do the same.

As you return to daily life, ask yourself:

If my life is a film, how would my Creative Optimum Self choose to show up in the next scene?

be passionate and grateful—
and life reveals its true beauty

Step Nine

Be Passionate and Grateful

As you begin to live your life with warmth and grace, you naturally become more passionate and grateful for life. You develop a genuine zest for living and bring a magnetic presence into each moment. Even when things do not unfold the way you hoped, you begin to understand that there are often hidden details at work, and that what appears disappointing in the moment may not serve your highest good in the long run. You feel safe and supported by life itself, even in moments of despair.

When you are not connected to your Creative Optimum Self, it is easy to fall into the trap of self-pity or depression. These are real and valid emotions at the human level—and they deserve compassion. However, when you learn to observe them from the soul level, as if you were watching your life unfold as a movie, you gain perspective and clarity through your deeper awareness.

In every experience, there is a lesson to be learned. When my father unexpectedly died at the age of fifty-seven, it marked one of the lowest points in my life. I was very close to him, even though I did not always agree with how he handled certain situations. Still, I deeply appreciated the goodness that existed within him. When he fell into a coma, my family was devastated. Doctors informed us that he would most likely remain in that state for the rest of his life; he was brain-dead. Because he had no living will, the decision to keep him on life support or remove the respirator was left to us. At first, it was an unbearable choice. As the days passed and he remained unresponsive, the decision slowly became clearer. His body did not move, yet tears streamed from his eyes. Those tears spoke to me. He was sad to be leaving this life, but he also seemed to know that letting go was the right thing for all of us.

Over time, I came to terms with his death and learned to appreciate life more deeply. I committed to living passionately, without regret. My father had regrets before he died—things he wished he had handled differently. He had lost his connection to his inner wisdom and passion for life. His passing became a powerful reminder for me to stay connected to mine.

Another experience illustrates this. In one chapter of my life, I was working on Wall Street for a major bank, earning a senior-level salary while living on Park Avenue in New York City. I traveled regularly to Europe on business and took frequent vacations to exotic destinations. From the outside, my life appeared ideal—and for a while, I believed it was. Eventually, I realized that my work was consuming me and that I was unhappy. I enjoyed the nature of the work itself, but I was not valued for what I produced. Ideas I presented were dismissed, only to be reused later by others to advance their own careers. My dissatisfaction began to affect my personal life. I stayed out late, neglected my health, and lived under constant stress. My blood pressure rose to dangerous levels. The breaking point came one evening after dinner with my girlfriend, when she unexpectedly proposed marriage. Though well-intended, we had never discussed this, and I was not ready. That same night, several others and I were struck with severe food poisoning. I ended up in the hospital, physically depleted and emotionally overwhelmed. When I returned home, I stayed up all night crying. I was deeply depressed, and in that stillness, I heard a quiet voice inside of me say, "Find me."

I listened. I left New York City and returned to my family home in New Jersey There, I picked up journaling again. Through writing, I realized that I was no longer living a passionate life. My work was not creative enough, and stress had blocked me from being truthful with myself. I had been raised by a mother who embodied creativity and zest for life, even through difficult times. I had lost that connection. That moment became a turning point—one that later fueled my transformation work and consulting practice.

By staying connected to your Creative Optimum Self, you naturally live a life of passion and bring that passion into everything you do. Some people remain in the same profession their entire lives, while others change paths or work across many industries. What matters is not the profession itself, but whether you feel alive in what you are doing. If you are not, your body and mind will eventually complain. Choose work that excites you, energizes you, and makes you feel fully alive. Passion aligns you with the flow of life, and in that flow, discovery unfolds naturally.

When you live passionately, gratitude follows. You begin to appreciate even the simplest moments—the air you breathe, the warmth of sunlight, a shared meal with loved ones. Gratitude shifts your perception and aligns you with universal love. It reminds you that while you are enjoying abundance, others may not be as fortunate, deepening compassion rather than guilt. Living a life of gratitude signals to the universal soul that you are open and ready for more. Opportunities begin to appear—sometimes unexpectedly—and often in ways you could not have planned. Life responds to awareness, appreciation, and presence. The universe itself operates with precision and harmony, sustaining life without effort or worry.

When you live passionately and gratefully, you align with that same intelligence. As more people do so, the world naturally moves toward greater harmony, peace, and balance. From that place, collaboration replaces competition, and shared purpose becomes possible. Gratitude and passion unite us and prepare us to improve the world—to build wisely, to serve responsibly, and to address our collective challenges with clarity and courage.

Recap

1. By living your life with passion, you follow the flow of life and engage fully with each experience. You live with fewer regrets and gain wisdom from everything you encounter.

2. You feel supported by life, trusting that when things do not go as planned, there is something meaningful to learn. With patience and insight, you find the path that brings harmony to you and others.

3. Gratitude deepens your connection to life. As you appreciate what you have and express enthusiasm in all that you do, you open yourself to new opportunities aligned with your Creative Optimum Self.

Exercise

This exercise has two parts.

Part One:

In your journal, make a list of all the things you are passionate about. For each passion, add one practical action you can take to express it. Assign a realistic date to each action and commit to following through. Completion restores clarity and momentum and ensures it does not become a loose end.

Part Two:

Write a gratitude list of everything you feel thankful for—your home, relationships, work, health, nature, simple moments. During meditation or journaling, revisit it and deepen your awareness of gratitude through visualization or writing.

As you practice gratitude daily, you align with the universal flow and the Integrated Being Intelligence. You open yourself to receive more and inspire others to do the same. In this shared alignment, awareness extends beyond the personal.

This exercise awakens alignment—the integration of passion, gratitude, and purposeful action.

As you reflect, ask yourself:

Where is my Creative Optimum Self already guiding me toward fuller expression, and what is the next small action that honors it?

your Creative Optimum Self

unfolds inwardly through

Integrated Being Intelligence

Step Ten

Becoming the Eyes and Ears of the Universe

As you live with passion and gratitude, and as the Inner and Outer Steps become integrated into your daily life, something subtle begins to change. You naturally start to live from your Creative Optimum Self. What I once described as becoming the "eyes and ears of the universe" can now be understood more clearly as awareness becoming aware of itself—your Creative Optimum Self expressing itself through Integrated Being Intelligence. This is no longer something you practice—it is who you are.

You are now aligned with an unseen and eternal intelligence that integrates all things into an orderly, coherent, and living whole. This intelligence becomes your inner guide. You trust it. You move with it. You no longer feel separate from life, but in relationship with it. You feel lighter, steadier, and safer in the world. Worry diminishes, fear loosens its grip, and a quiet confidence takes its place. You know—not intellectually, but deeply—that you are part of something meaningful. You sense your connection with both the seen and unseen dimensions of existence.

Beauty reveals itself everywhere. In plants, animals, people, oceans, skies, and simple moments, inspiration becomes constant. You awaken to a world you may not have known existed before. Smiling comes more easily. Laughter flows naturally. And this joy extends outward—touching others without effort. Your concern expands beyond your immediate circle. You care for strangers as naturally as friends. You feel compelled to support, guide, and protect life where it is vulnerable. You stand for truth without aggression, with clarity rather than force. There is a quiet fearlessness in you—not the bravado of ego, but the steadiness of someone aligned with wisdom. You move through life with elegance and civility. You see and hear things others may overlook. Patterns, connections, and subtle signals become visible.

Over time, perception itself deepens. You begin to see beyond what the eyes alone can register—whether open or closed. You see light in both brightness and shadow; love in both kindness and brokenness. You begin to see what the universe sees. Where others see failure, you perceive opportunity. Where others see problems, you recognize solutions. Where others are anchored in the past, you sense what is emerging.

You glimpse a world that does not yet fully exist—one free of violence, hatred, discrimination, and injustice— and you know it is possible. People are drawn to you. Differences soften in your presence. Your openness dissolves division, not through argument, but through coherence. There is a magnetism about you that others recognize intuitively. They see in you a way of being they long for themselves. As they spend time with you, they feel inspired—not pressured—to live with greater grace, love, and harmony. They begin to sense what a loving, inspiring, fulfilling existence can feel like.

As you continue to live from your soul, your awareness of life's signals sharpens. You begin to hear the universe speak—not in words alone, but through experiences, relationships, and timing. Guidance arrives naturally. Answers come while walking by the sea, watching a film or speaking with a stranger. Information appears at the right moment—through a conversation, a headline, a passing remark. You think of someone, and they call. You consider a decision, and clarity presents itself through unexpected channels. These are not coincidences. They are signs of coherence.

Your soul is now in relationship with the universal soul. There is trust. You ask and receive. As you give love, harmony, and attention to life, life responds in kind. You are no longer reacting to the world—you are co-creating it. Living from this place provides abundant energy. Focus sharpens. Precision increases. You move through work, conversation, rest, and even sleep with presence. Dreams become clearer, more meaningful, and connected to waking life. You excel not by striving, but by being fully present. In moments of deep connection—with another person, with creativity, with nature—experience transcends the physical. Silence becomes full. Bliss arises without effort. You touch the intelligence of the moment itself, where wisdom and energy are already complete.

The same is true for intention. Ideas written in a journal, visions held in meditation, creative impulses honored with patience—when aligned with your Creative Optimum Self, they find their way into form. Intentions become messages to the unseen field, and when coherence is present, reality responds. As creativity is infused into the world, harmony expands. Life organizes itself more gracefully.

As you continue to live with the eyes and ears of the universe, you recognize that what has transformed is not the world alone—it is you. The body that houses this integrated being begins to feel lighter, energized, and alive. You are joyful not because life is perfect, but because you are present. Fear of death dissolves, replaced by understanding. You recognize that while the body changes and eventually fades, awareness and wisdom are not bound by form. Life and death are movements within a greater continuity.

The Earth spins at extraordinary speed—unseen, yet perfectly balanced. Existence operates beyond what the senses can register. At its foundation, all things are made of the same energy—swirling, interconnecting, overlapping in a vast and intricate dance. When you experience moments that feel miraculous, deeply connected, or beyond explanation, recognize them for what they are. Something subtle yet profound occurs.

You are no longer only aware of life—you become aware of awareness itself. You recognize that the observer, the experience, and life itself are no longer separate. Awareness becomes aware of its own presence.

You are witnessing the living expression of Integrated Being Intelligence.

Recap

1. By living from your Creative Optimum Self, you embody Integrated Being Intelligence—an awakened state of presence where peace, clarity, and harmony guide your thoughts, words, and actions. You see beauty in all life and respond from truth rather than fear.

2. You become attuned to the seen and unseen dimensions of existence. Wisdom, insight, and guidance are available in every moment, and you trust the intelligence of life itself. You no longer fear uncertainty—or even death—because you understand continuity beyond form.

3. As the eyes and ears of the universe, you serve life through awareness, compassion, and coherence. Your

presence alone inspires others to awaken, and through embodied love, the world begins to transform—one conscious being at a time.

Exercise

This is a visual awareness exercise designed to expand perception and cultivate embodied presence. Prepare yourself as you would for meditation. Sit comfortably and bring your attention to your breath until the mind becomes still.

Now imagine that you are the lens of a camera observing reality. See yourself through this lens exactly as you are in this moment—your posture, your expression, the room around you. Slowly allow the lens to move, capturing your surroundings in detail: your home, familiar spaces, objects, textures, and light. Let the lens move beyond your home—into your building, your neighborhood, your workplace, your community. Observe faces, movement, life unfolding.

Now allow the lens to travel further—across your city, your country, nature, oceans, landscapes, and places you have known. Continue outward, effortlessly, until you are observing the world as a whole, and then beyond—into the stars.

Hold all of these images gently in awareness. Offer them your attention. Offer them love. Remain here for a few moments. When you feel complete, slowly return and open your eyes.

With practice, this exercise trains you to move through life as conscious awareness itself—seeing, hearing, and blessing reality as it unfolds. You begin to anticipate harmony rather than conflict, solutions rather than problems, healing rather than separation.

In this way, you become the eyes and ears of the universe—and through your presence, life responds.

This exercise awakens embodied presence—awareness recognizing itself across inner and outer worlds.

As you return, affirm:

Today I recognize that I am aware of my own awareness, and I move through the world blessing the life around me.

Transformation
takes you to heaven on earth.

Conclusion

Creative Optimum Self is not a destination. It is an ongoing journey—a living intelligence—a way of being, perceiving, and engaging with life.

The journey begins inward. You learn to observe yourself honestly, to journal, reflect, and gradually release the conditioned layers that once shaped your perceptions. Through meditation, inspiration, and presence, you reconnect with your inner guide—the quiet intelligence that has always lived within you. You begin to care for the body as a vessel of awareness, recognizing that clarity of mind and coherence of soul flourish through well-being, rhythm, and respect for life. As inner alignment deepens, your life naturally expands outward. You complete what you begin, bringing order, integrity, and lightness into your daily experience. Relationships become a place of learning, connection, and shared growth. Warmth and grace emerge naturally as part of your presence. Passion and gratitude flow through your actions, energizing creativity, purpose, and service.

Over time, a deeper realization unfolds. You begin to recognize awareness itself—the quiet presence behind every experience. The observer, the experience, and life itself reveal their connection within a greater field of intelligence, where patterns become visible and coherence deepens with greater clarity. Guidance emerges in ways that once seemed subtle or unseen. You live with the eyes and ears of the universe—the living expression of Integrated Being Intelligence.

Integrated Being Intelligence describes how awareness lives within the human experience—through the body, emotions, mind, relationships, and connection to Source. Together, these dimensions form a coherent field of being from which clarity, harmony, and wise action arise.

As this inner coherence expresses itself in the world—through the way we relate, decide, and serve—it naturally expands into Integrated Leadership Intelligence. Leadership emerges as a way of living: grounded in awareness, guided by responsibility, and expressed through compassion and wisdom.

This journey continues to unfold—alive in every step you take.

The Five Dimensions

of *Integrated Being Intelligence*

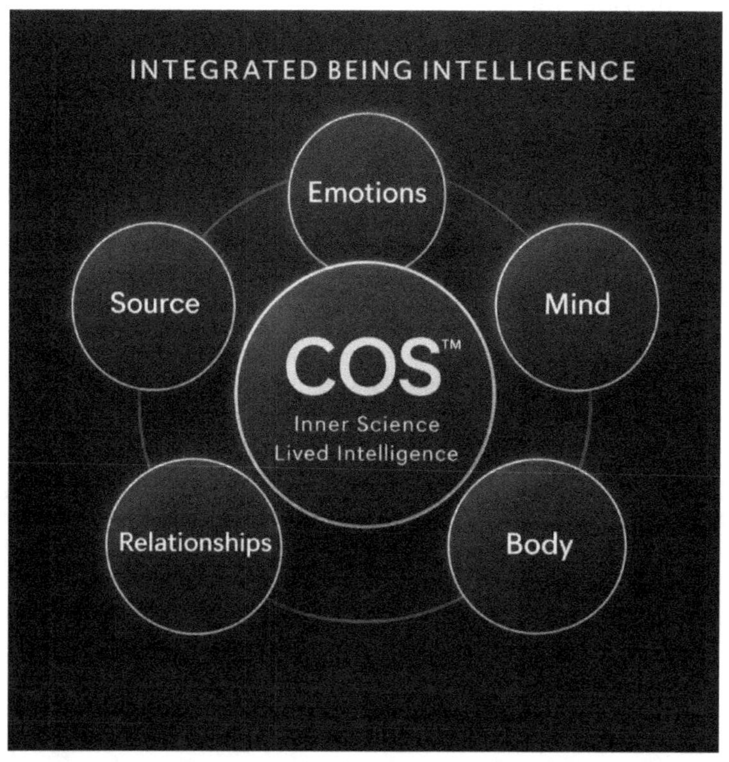

Source • Mind • Emotions • Body • Relationships

When these dimensions operate in coherence, the Creative Optimum Self emerges naturally.

Final Note

As I complete this book, I want to leave you with this understanding.

Creative Optimum Self is my living philosophy.

In my companion volume, *48 Answers for My Son: An Architecture of Integrated Leadership Intelligence*, I share how this practice has emerged through living it and how I have evolved along the way.

This is a living practice and a never-ending journey. As you apply the Inner Steps faithfully, you evolve and are guided to execute the Outer Steps intuitively.

You begin to see your life with greater clarity. You become more aware of how you think, how you feel, and how you respond.

You become aware of awareness itself.

As this awareness matures, you begin to embody the integration of all dimensions—body, mind, emotions, relationships, and Source.

You become the witness, and you live as Integrated Being Intelligence.

And from there, life continues to unfold—expanding, refining, and evolving through every moment.

COS—A Timeless Orientation

I am infinite intelligence in expression.

I operate as the Creative Optimum Self,

integrating inner and outer worlds,

being and leadership,

the seen and the unseen.

I live with awareness—

aware of awareness itself.

This is COS—and this is The Way.

About the Author

Costantino Delli is a leadership architect, coach, author, and founder of the COS (Creative Optimum Self) Philosophy—an integrated system uniting Integrated Being Intelligence and Integrated Leadership Intelligence. His work bridges inner mastery with operational excellence, helping individuals and leaders integrate who they are with how they think, decide, act, and serve.

Born in Taranto, Italy, Delli immigrated to the United States at the age of eight. Early experiences shaped by hospitality, mathematics, storytelling, and adversity formed the foundation of a philosophy grounded in precision, empathy, and human-centered responsibility.

Delli began his career in finance and systems engineering, working across banking, defense analytics, and global financial markets, where precision, reliability, and disciplined execution became foundational to his leadership philosophy. A professional and personal breakdown became the catalyst for the inner transformation that would shape his life's work.

Over time, Delli articulated the Creative Optimum Self, integrating inner awareness with creative expression and disciplined execution. From this foundation emerged two complementary expressions of the same intelligence: Integrated Being Intelligence, which describes how intelligence is lived internally through awareness, embodiment, and presence, and Integrated Leadership Intelligence, which describes how that same intelligence is expressed externally through thinking, relating, organizing, and serving in the world. Together, they form one coherent system expressed across dimensions: being and doing, inner and outer, awareness and application.

He founded COS 4 Excellence, advising organizations across finance, media, and technology on leadership architecture, enterprise transformation, and integrated human–system performance. He later extended the COS framework through COS AI Mirror— a proprietary conscious framework enabling leaders to develop intelligence aligned with their values, voice, and lived wisdom.

Over the course of his career, Delli has worked across finance, technology, media, entertainment, healthcare, and consulting, contributing to the design and transformation of complex systems and advising leaders in environments where clarity, trust, and performance are inseparable. Across all expressions, his work remains guided by the COS Philosophy—one intelligence, lived fully, within and without.

Delli's first book, *The Way: Live Your Dream, It's Not a Secret!*—now evolved into *Creative Optimum Self: Transform Your Life and Your World*—introduced a framework of five inner and five outer steps for service and leadership excellence.

His second book, *48 Answers for My Son: An Architecture of Integrated Leadership Intelligence*, expresses the lived architecture of leadership, responsibility, and execution through reflection and experience.

He currently resides in California.

Continue the Architecture

Creative Optimum Self explores the inner dimension of transformation—coherence, discipline, and the process of becoming aware of awareness itself.

For the lived, cinematic expression of these principles in leadership, responsibility, and execution, continue with:

48 Answers for My Son: An Architecture of Integrated Leadership Intelligence

The journey inward and the journey outward are one intelligence, lived inwardly and expressed outwardly as a unified way of being.

Future works will explore how the Creative Optimum Self can be cultivated in education, integrated into organizations, and applied to broader social challenges.

A portion of the net proceeds from this book supports the development of COS 4 LIFE, a mission dedicated to fostering Loving, Inspiring, Fulfilling Existence—personally and collectively.

Because when individuals awaken their Creative Optimum Self, communities strengthen, leadership matures, and meaningful change becomes possible.

Learn more: www.cosphilosophy.com

9 780979 623721